What Pe

"*Return to Happiness* has the power to help individuals focus on their true purpose and reach for the best in life through helping others."

— Somaly Mam, CNN Hero and Best-Selling Author of *The Road to Lost Innocence*

"Ryan's journey is truly unique and inspiring! His story will touch you in a special way and will inspire you to intensify your connection with the power within you to enjoy greater happiness, go for your dreams, and find total peace."

— Peggy McColl, New York Times Best-Selling Author of *The Best Seller Maker*

"*Return to Happiness* is all about inspiration and so much more. Ryan's journey will help you understand the struggles we all face in our daily journey. Use this book as a tool for success and, of course, happiness."

— Joe Nunziata, Best-Selling Author of *Spiritual Selling* and *Karma Buster*

"If there's one thing that's true to human nature, it's that we're all searching for that thing...that little piece of something that makes our hearts beat faster, our eyes get wider, and our lives feel richer...and sometimes it's just the gentle nudge of a friend who reminds us that that little something has been here all along.... May this book be the nudging friend you needed."

— Andrew Allen, Sony Records

"This is a powerful masterpiece.... *Return to Happiness* will literally transform your life. Ryan's journey will truly show you the magic of how anything can happen when guided by faith."

— Chris Messenger, Author of *Think it Write it Live it*

"Ryan never slips silently into anyone's life. He makes an entrance! And the impact felt is always extreme. In *Return to Happiness*, that impact explodes upon the world! Seeking, searching, challenging.... Who am I? Why I am I here? What is my purpose? The openness with which Ryan's story is shared is the catalyst that binds. There is but one of us, knowing and touching all! This message is a glimpse into the vision of each one who walks this planet, binding us inevitably to each other in our constant journey to return to happiness!"

— Jim McKillop, Author of *Notes from Papa*

RETURN TO HAPPINESS

Ryan's Journey

Ryan John Phillips

ISBN:194362545X
ISBN-13:9781943625451

DEDICATION

To My Family

I love you....THANK YOU!

"The cave you fear to enter, holds the treasures you seek."
— Joseph Campbell.

CONTENTS

Acknowledgments....................i
Foreword....................iii
PART I: ADVERSITY....................v
Chapter 1 My Bad Decision....................1
Chapter 2 THE TEST....................11
Chapter 3 Reassessing My Past....................16
Chapter 4 Prison and New Beliefs....................26
Chapter 5 Inception of *Return to Happiness*....................37
Chapter 6 Bangkok—The Journey Begins....................56
Chapter 7 Khao Lak—Experiencing Love....................60
Chapter 8 Patong—Health....................65
Chapter 9 Phi Phi—The Simplicity of Life....................72
Chapter 10 Luang Prabang—The Universal Mind....................85
Chapter 11 Siem Reap, Cambodia....................98
Chapter 12 Phnom Penh, Cambodia....................105
Chapter 13 The Ride and Giving Back....................112
Chapter 14 Chiang Mai—Freedom....................125
Chapter 15 Happiness....................130
PART II: DIVIDENDS....................137
Chapter 1 A Fortuitous Flight....................139
Chapter 2 In La La Land....................142
Chapter 3 New York City—The Center of the World....................149
Chapter 4 Vancouver—The Last Leg of Completion....................153
Chapter 5 The Miami Premiere and a Film Festival....................160
Chapter 6 Agape—Unconditional Love....................168
Chapter 7 Car Troubles and Divine Order....................178
Chapter 8 Genshai Life Mastery Retreat....................185
Conclusion New Beginnings without End....................199
About The Author....................205

ACKNOWLEDGMENTS

In the course of my life, I have passed by millions of souls all over the world. If it weren't for the love and support of my family, I wouldn't have had or continue to have the continuous opportunity to help others. From the days when my parents, Grant and Cindy, would drive me to countless hockey games and practices, plus many other sporting events, through their unconditional love and support during my days in prison and the underworld, I am truly blessed. I wrote this book to show that with positive intention, anything we dream about, we can bring forth into reality. My daughter Sadie is a driving force whom I admire for her strength and courage through all the days I couldn't be there for her. This book is for humanity and a more harmonious world built on love and compassion. I was only the channel that expressed these words. There are too many people to thank by name—I could fill pages upon pages—but you know who you are...my friends whom I've met and who have stood by me through thick and thin and my editor, Tyler Tichelaar, who helped me achieve what you are about to read. To all the people who were there for me in my hockey days, the countless players, coaches, and business owners who made us feel at home, even when we were so far away. To all my brothers whom I met in prison, and the underworld, I wish you safety and protection, for your life is worth it. I want to say a special thanks to all the riders who traversed across Cambodia and Vietnam on two separate occasions. Raising awareness about sex slavery has changed my life. To all the people in the world who deserve to be free, you have my infinite blessings. I promise never to give up in my quest to make this world a better place.

"Through my adversity, I found my authenticity."
— Ryan John Phillips

RYAN JOHN PHILLIPS

FOREWORD

I have always been a big fan of the Buddha. His simple, yet powerful words have always resonated with me. One of the Buddha's teachings is based on the fact that we must acknowledge this: in life, there is suffering and pain. Although his work was focused on ending suffering, he knew acceptance was the key.

This book is about hope and dreams, but the story is filled with struggle. The human experience contains many twists and turns. Each experience helps us elevate our consciousness to a higher level.

Let Ryan's story serve as more than a lesson. It will show you how the human spirit can overcome any obstacles and challenges. In the end, it is not about where you come from but where you go that matters most.

You too can be an inspiration to others by your daily words and actions. We all face many challenges in this life. Having the courage to move forward and continue the journey is the difference between success and a life of what might have been.

I ask you to turn to the story in this book and see yourself in it. There is a little part of you in Ryan's journey. You are here to soar to new heights. Now it is time to allow yourself to be great.

Joe Nunziata

RYAN JOHN PHILLIPS

PART I: ADVERSITY

CHAPTER 1
MY BAD DECISION

"Every adversity, every failure, every heartache carries with it the seed of an equal or greater benefit."
— Napoleon Hill

As I lay face down on the side of the Mount Baker Highway with guns pointed at my head, I knew I had made a horrible mistake. It was September 17, 2000, and the decision I had made would impact me and all the people I loved for a long time to come. My whole life flashed before my eyes in that moment. I looked to my right as the left side of my head felt the cold gravel against my face. I was scared to death about what the outcome of this situation would be. My partners in crime and I had just been pulled out of our car by the United States Drug Enforcement Agency (DEA). Before long, the canine unit showed up with what sounded like at least three dogs. I couldn't see them since my head was plastered to the ground, but I knew they would find in the trunk the 103 pounds of high grade marijuana from British Columbia, Canada. I looked over and saw one of the officers waving his hand over his nose while smiling at his associates. The dogs were barking loudly. And when I heard the trunk open, I watched the team of undercover officers high-fiving like they had just won the lottery—they had just seen the four knapsacks containing the shipment.

I was about to learn real fast that there is no such reality as something for nothing in this life. Not only that, but I was in the midst of the most paralyzing fear I had ever known. Fear is what I've always feared the most! Fear of fear—fear of the unknown. When fear grips you, it can totally take over your mind and physical body, making it hard to reason or have any hope for the future. I had now plunged into a deep level of despair.

My intuition the night before had told me I was making a mistake. I should have listened to my gut, but my emotions were all over the place. In the previous three weeks leading up to this fateful moment, I had put myself into some very threatening situations. I was "involved," and my involvement had become more than just that of a backseat driver in the business. I had wanted to be the man. I had something to prove to the world...that I wasn't a failure. I thought money would make me a man of power, and the booming marijuana trade in BC offered what I thought was easy money.

I associated myself with gangsters, and on some level, I thought it was cool to do so. I felt I had some sort of power from being surrounded by people in the underworld. Maybe subconsciously, I wanted an identity where people would respect me out of fear and for what I could accumulate materially. I didn't know the severity of the ramifications if I were busted on the United States' side of the border. During the day, I would try my best to mastermind the business, and at night, I was a rock star at the clubs. From the time I was sixteen, I had thought I was a somebody because I could walk through any line up at any club in the city. If I couldn't walk right in, I could slip the doorman a bill and instantly my crew would be waited on hand and foot because the club employees knew we were big spenders. I had played this role fueled by my ego and desire to be somebody in the world. Now, apprehended by the authorities on the other side of the border, the price for having that ego was going to be the loss of my freedom.

From the time I was a little boy, I had always had this deep inner sense that everything happens for a reason; nothing ever happens by mere chance or luck. In my mind, there are no accidents. Every decision and choice we make in life always has an outcome. The law of cause and effect is responsible for everything in our lives, and knowing that, I now realized I would pay the ultimate price.

I was a new father to a beautiful one-year old daughter named Sadie. The day she was born had been the best day of my life even though I was very immature and unprepared to be a father. On that day, there was a massive storm, and Sadie's mom was in painful labor for over sixteen hours; during the last few hours, she was given an epidermal shot to relieve some of the harsh pain. Finally, by the grace of God, our beautiful little girl was born at 12:13 a.m. on July 10, 1999.

Right as Sadie was born, the storm ended, and I remember looking up into the air with tears streaming down my face as I heard Sadie's first sound, a loud cry. The reality now hit home big time—I was a parent!

That day, I couldn't have handled myself any more inappropriately. Don't get me wrong—I was the proudest father in the world. But having a bunch of my hockey buddies there in the birth care center, drinking large amounts of champagne and whiskey, didn't impress Sadie's mother or grandmother. I actually kept it together somewhat, but I thought this was a time for celebration.

After everyone left, it was just the three of us now experiencing the breath of a new life in the world. That was a long night. I remember changing Sadie's first diaper. I felt such a sense of peace come over me, like I actually had contributed something positive to the world. Wichita is three hours ahead of Vancouver, so if Sadie had been born in Canada, she would have been born on July 9th. I was born on July 8th. Her mom was born July 11th, so we were all Cancers. They say we Cancers are sensitive types, whoever "they" are, and I think they're right. True story: my mom was in labor for exactly the same amount of time as Sadie's mom, and there was a massive storm that evening also, while the next day there wasn't a cloud in the sky! When I left the birth care center early the next morning to go grab some clothes and gifts, I couldn't see a cloud in the baby blue sky. Maybe it was just a coincidence, but this I do know: Whoever you make your god out to be, he or she works in mysterious ways.

Sadie's birth gave me a new lease on life. I was determined to make fatherhood work. I had a video recorder at the hospital where my buddy filmed me talking in the hallway, trying to contain my emotions five minutes before Sadie entered the world. On that video, I told my daughter, "Sadie, I'm your dad, and I will always be here for you. I will always love you no matter what, and you will be brought up with values because that's what I believe in." After Sadie was born, I held her in my arms; she was so tiny, and I could feel the pure love radiating from her being. As my buddy filmed me, I said, "This is honestly the best day of my life; you are in this world, and you are going to make a lot of difference. I LOVE YOU!"

Shortly after, and against Sadie's mom's family's wishes, my daughter and her mother came to visit me in Canada. I couldn't blame the family one bit for how they felt because they knew all too well the illegal activities I was involved in. They tried talking to me, but I wouldn't listen to a word anyone had to say. I was stubborn and set in my ways. I felt that hockey had failed me, and this drug trafficking business was a chance to elevate me into the high brackets of society through large sums of quick cash. The mother of my child soon realized her family had been right. Sadie and she returned to the States, leaving me to my wild ways. I became a lonely monster, driven by greed and status.

I've often wondered when the turning point toward such selfishness occurred in my life. When had I made my decision to go against the grain of society? In my mind, I had convinced myself that it was "only pot" and "The government is against people getting ahead in life." I had all the excuses made up in my mind. I wasn't a violent man, so what problems would I ever face? One of my friends, who was making a good amount of money, loved my wild party ways and energetic personality, and since he made good money, I figured I could finally arrive by doing the same. I was Ryan, the wild party guy who could make anyone laugh.

I love laughter and firmly believe it's the best medicine available to man. Today, the only jokes I make are at my own expense. But back then, I was so judgmental. Now I believe that to judge someone else is actually to judge yourself.

In 1997, I had started off the year playing hockey in Louisiana. I got off to a great start, considering I had only skated a handful of times that summer. I was twenty-two years old and my body was very resilient.

That summer was spent hanging out with my new "bros," and it consisted of wild parties, after-hours clubs, and raves. One of my friends had the drug ecstasy being shipped in from San Francisco, so every night when we went out, our pockets were full of "MDMA pills." We thought we were cool—that we had "it all." I did enough of the drug that summer that I'm surprised my brain didn't turn into mush. But it was the pure stuff! That's what made it okay—because we knew the source.

I still had hockey as a career goal. I couldn't let my parents down; a part of me really cared what they thought at that point. Then four games into the season, I broke my hand. I was leading my team in scoring and full of confidence in Shreveport, Louisiana. Only a few minutes were left in the game when I took a vicious slash to my left hand below my pinky finger and the bone broke in half. Pins were inserted the next day and I was out of commission for three months. I remember waking up after surgery to a nice nurse whom I asked on a date for that evening; the rookie party was that night and I wasn't going to miss it for the world.

The doctor gave me some pain killers, and I popped a few as soon as my ride showed up. I don't remember the ride home, but I do remember waking up on my kitchen floor. I still made the party, though, and I drank my sorrows away. The nurse showed up for a quick minute, saw the behavior going on, and I never saw her face again. By then, I was seeing Sadie's mom, but I wasn't being faithful.

That time could have been spent more constructively. Instead, I chose to party hard! I took a fourteen-hour road trip to Green Bay with one of my teammates who was also out of the lineup with a broken hand. His girlfriend was going to school there at Saint Norbert's College. We stopped off at the University of Wisconsin and grabbed an ounce of indoor weed for our trip. I fit right into the frat life all right, and since it was Oktoberfest, oh boy, it was my time to shine, and I made friends easily. We stayed at my buddy's old frat house and went hard for three days straight. I was dared to saw off my cast at a keg party that weekend. A student got over a hundred people to chant, "Take it off! Take it off!" and so I did. Big mistake. My hand was black and blue, and the pins stuck out of the side. A nice girl handed me some duct tape so I could fix the damage that I had inflicted on myself. People were laughing away, and I was feeling like a real fool, although heavily intoxicated.

I tried to hide my hand from my coach when I got back to Louisiana, but word had already gotten out. "How stupid can you be?" he asked. I told him my cast had been itchy so

I had to take it off, but one of my teammates snitched the whole story to him. When I was finally ready to play again, my coach couldn't have traded me any faster. I ended up being traded to Waco, Texas, the last place team. That trade made me bitter! He traded me on a day when Waco played in Louisiana, so I was told to have all my stuff packed, play against my old team that night, and then make the eleven-hour bus ride back to Texas. My new Waco team won the game in overtime. I made it my mission to play my heart out in Waco to prove to my former coach that he had made a mistake. I was on fire when I first joined my new team, but I soon chose to walk down the dark path again. With only a few games left in the season, I missed practice because I was high on cocaine. I didn't call the coach; I just didn't show. That was it! I was benched for the last two games.

Then I got a call from my buddies back home, inviting me to go with them to spring break in Cancun—"the biggest party of the year." In retrospect, Cancun may have been the turning point in my life. I got a lift from one of my teammates in Waco to meet my friends from Vancouver in Houston where there was a connector flight. I had no idea what to expect in Cancun, other than my buddies telling me it would be partying on "another level." We slammed back Coronas while we waited for our flight to board. I know I downed at least a dozen. That was the start of a fourteen-day alcohol and drug bender, during which I maybe only slept twenty-four hours.

During the day, the party was on Oasis Beach. Over 500,000 college kids were on the Yucatan Peninsula, and most had left their morals at home. I had never seen anything like it. My friends had an endless supply of cash. Our crew stuck out like sore thumbs on the beach and in the night clubs. One of my friends went so far as to make business cards saying, "Spelling Productions Head Talent Scout." He would entice girls by giving them his card and telling them they were "perfect for the next movie." He had his Versace shades on, a gold and diamond Rolex, and a big gold chain. I just shook my head, but I thought it was all fun now, and no rules!

We would stroll into La Boom, the biggest club there with a line-up two blocks down the street to get in, but when the door men saw us, their eyes would light up because we were their best customers. When we walked in, they would announce over the mic, "Welcome, our good friends from Beverly Hills" because my one pal had told a white lie that we came from the Hills. The second we got in, we were escorted into the VIP lounge. Tables would be placed in front of us loaded with endless bottles of Dom Pérignon and Cristal, vodka, and beer. We attracted all the girls because we gave away free drinks and ecstasy. If we put a cigarette in our mouths, a lighter from one of the staff was there in a second to light it. I thought to myself, "This is the big time; this is what money can do!" Cold steam would shoot down from the roof, and I don't think there was one night we didn't close that place down. When we would walk out of the club at 8 a.m., the sun would hurt our half-shut eyes. Shirts off or wide open, we would go from there to the beach, then do it all over again the next night.

I wanted this lifestyle that seemed so glamorous on the surface. As clear as day, I remember having a conversation on the last night there before returning to Vancouver that if we died that night, our lives would have been fulfilled. That's where my mind was. And while I didn't get dragged into the drug business, I was more or less guided in because of the people I associated myself with.

I remember being on the plane back, my nerves shot from so many chemicals and cocktails. And the party was just getting started because as soon as we got home, we just kept the ball rolling and flew off to Vegas a few days later. I started learning how the business worked and educated myself on what I would have to do in order to be successful—as I measured success at that time. My friends had boats and fancy cars, so if I didn't have the same, I felt I would be left out and going without. But neither was I ready yet to give up on hockey. "One more year," I told myself, although I had to deflect a lot of my friends' arguments about wanting to leave. I was making money now, much more than my $400 a week salary playing hockey. I went to Topeka as a twenty-three-year old with a cocky attitude because I was living the so-called "high life" now instead of just the boring, simple life of a struggling hockey player in the minor leagues.

But I got into the hockey life again. I had always respected the majority of my teammates, and up to that point, playing on a team is what had taught me the most about my own character, making me realize that in order to win, we all needed to be on the same page, with our desires working in a spirit of harmony. If there were too many weak links in the chain, then the obvious outcome would be a loss.

That year while I played in Topeka, my girlfriend became pregnant. I was full of fear about being a father, and I was hard on myself; I actually told myself that since she was pregnant, this time would be my last hoorah before having to grow up and assume the role of a parent. My coach really cared about me and was worried about how I was abusing my body off the ice. He would pull me into his office and tell me wholeheartedly how I could turn my situation into a positive. He gave me sound advice, but I chose to play the victim. The birth of my child would be life's greatest blessing for me, but in the months leading up to that birth, I felt like there was a force against me.

That's the thing about the universe—it wants us to succeed most of the time. It doesn't want to push us around. The universe actually is made up of energy governed by our thoughts, so when we control our thoughts, rather than letting them control us, we can demand exactly how our lives should go. But I didn't realize that at the time, so my life reflected only the negative thought-energy I was radiating.

Finally, my coach got fed up! Not only was I leading myself down the wrong path, but I was bringing others with me. I was a natural leader and could convince anyone to follow me. When I got traded that season to San Antonio, Texas at the trade deadline, I refused to go. Instead, I took off back to Cancun for spring break. Great choice while my daughter was in the womb. I got the nickname "Ryan South." I hadn't yet learned that "Quitters never win!" Hockey was over for me now, so I could go home and join my friends in really getting ahead in life. I saw a door opening for me to an abundant life—what an illusion.

Whenever we go through any adversity in life, and most of us will go through many, we may ask ourselves, "Where is the seed to an equal or greater benefit from this experience?" The answer always lies inside us; you can either accept whatever has brought you down to hold you in that state of mind, or you can use the adversity as motivation. That's where the seed lies, and it's up to us to make the seed grow by the actions we perform, by realizing that failure is only permanent if we allow it to be. At this point of my life, I was young and the word *adversity* had no meaning whatsoever.

CHAPTER 2
THE TEST

After being put into handcuffs, I was led into a vehicle that would be transporting us to the United States border patrol station for questioning. The first thing I asked the officer in the front seat was "Will I ever be allowed back into the U.S.?" His definite "NO!" hit me like a ton of bricks.

My mind was spinning out of control and I wanted to cry, but I had to stay strong; I could only envision how my baby girl would now be brought up without a father. And what would my parents say? "This isn't supposed to be happening to me," I thought. But at the same time, I felt a sense of relief; perhaps a higher purpose existed for why I had been caught. I realized now that I had been going down a dark path with alcohol and drugs for some time; maybe this was God's way of stopping me in my tracks with a serious wake-up call. I was far from happy at this point in my life. I had just turned twenty-four and let a once very promising hockey career slip away from me through my actions off the ice and by not believing in myself. I had come to expect only failure and attracted it through my negative thoughts. I had lost that inner child who'd had big dreams, even though I knew anything was possible in this world if I could form a clear mental picture of what I wanted.

A big steel gate opened and the vehicle I was in proceeded to drive into the border protection headquarters of Whatcom County. My heart was sinking inside of me as I realized my freedom was going to be taken away from me for a long time. The five people who had been involved with me were all scared, wet, and dirty from a long seven-hour hike through the mountains that day. An old logging road on the Canadian side of the border had connected a long bushwhacked trail through rough terrain. That had been our gateway into the United States with our contraband.

Once in the border protection headquarters, all five of us were thrown into a small cell where we looked at each other with fear and uncertainty. I was willing to take full responsibility for my actions, but this was a hard pill to swallow when the future was unknown. My one burning question was "How long will we be in prison?" The main officer who had apprehended us was being very polite to us; obviously he wanted information about who owned the product and where it was all going.

I was steadfast in my determination not to reveal any information to the authorities, and I made it clear to my codefendants that they should keep their mouths shut as well. I had made some really bad decisions up to this point, but the one thing I wasn't was a snitch. We all had to give statements at the border patrol center, and I kept mine brief.... I was being paid to smuggle twenty-five pounds of marijuana across the border—period. I obviously knew people back home who were involved in "the business," but there were growers, middle men, distributors, etc.—it was one of BC's biggest industries at that time! Even up there with lumber. But I was the one who had made the choice to do what I did, and I wasn't about to take anyone down with me.

At first, I heard my sentence was likely to be five years minimum. Then, once we got escorted to the county jail, where everyone in my small pod of offenders had committed different crimes, I heard every story in the book from two years to ten years. I didn't know whom to believe, but I'd watched enough movies and television in my time to know not to trust anybody!

After being given an orange jumpsuit and getting fingerprinted, the hardest part of that first night was calling my dad. My first words to him were, "Dad, I'm in big trouble! I'm in jail in the States." At first, my dad actually thought I was joking, even though he had to accept a collect call from Whatcom County Jail. After a brief pause, he could sense the serious tone in my voice. I was far from joking! He was devastated, and he told me that my mom would be coming to see me the next day.

That was a largely sleepless night. The walls in my small 8' x 12' cell were covered with gang signs and the names of previous inmates. I will never forget one of the sayings that was carved into the white paint. "Welcome to hell!" That statement pretty much summed up how I was feeling. And the road ahead of me didn't seem too bright.

Wake-up call was at 6 a.m. the next morning with breakfast served on pink plastic trays. I hadn't eaten in almost two days, so the sloppy oatmeal and dry white toast tasted like a gourmet meal. The sad reality was setting in now—I was in a cage and going nowhere! Not a good feeling for me since I had suffered from claustrophobia since I was young. The pod I was in consisted of only eight jail cells. And the only thing I had in common with the other inmates, besides being human, was that I had broken the law. Coming from an honest, hardworking family that had brought me up with values, this crime was totally out of character for me. But I had seen the surface of what large sums of money could bring (temporary happiness), and I had wanted what the people I'd been associating with had. I had always wanted to be a success in life, so after hockey hadn't worked out as planned, I had pursued what I thought was an opportunity to quick riches. And naive about organized crime, I had gotten myself in way over my head.

Later that first day in jail, my mom and my brother Greg showed up to see me. I'll never forget the way my mom looked at me, her firstborn, with tears of disappointment in her eyes. I could sense that she felt somewhat responsible and was probably asking herself, "Where did I go wrong?" I assured her I was okay and that my safety wasn't an issue. My brother didn't know what to say since he had always looked up to me as a role model. I told my mom that I needed a lawyer, but I didn't want my parents to spend a dime. I asked her to get me a public defender because they were free. I had gotten myself into this mess, so I would have to be the one to ride it out, no matter how long the justice system was going to give me. Mom told me that she had felt something was terribly wrong the night before I was arrested. She had always had a way of knowing when things were bad for me—call it a mother's instinct or sixth sense.

Telling Sadie's mom was one of the toughest things I ever had to do. I had put her through a lot and she knew what I was up to. She was only twenty-one, and even though we had broken up nearly six months earlier, we still had a close bond because of our daughter. After she accepted the collect call from the jail, I stuttered on the phone and then confessed. I told her, " I'm so sorry; I've let so many people down; you were right, and now I'm paying the price you told me I would." Her exact words were a tearful, "I knew it!" But for some reason, she always had a way of showing compassion, and said, "No matter what, I will be there for you, and nothing will ever change the fact that Sadie is your daughter." I told her, "I'm so sorry, and I vow to make this right." Then I had to drop the bomb on her that I might never again have the privilege of being allowed access to the United States. A long silence overcame us both. Then she said she was sorry that this was all happening; "Why me?" she asked and then hung up. Obviously, the self-inflicted misery that I had caused for everyone who mattered in my life was becoming more than just a bad dream; it was a nightmare I couldn't wake up from if I tried.

I was guilty, and there was no way out of the situation other than to go with the flow and take what was handed to me step-by-step through the legal process. My time in prison would end up being the most humbling time of my life and a time for serious self-introspection.

CHAPTER 3
REASSESSING MY PAST

As I was experiencing these events, I was overcome by memories of my childhood and how I had been raised to have values. How had I let slip away everything I had been raised to believe and stand for? I mean, I was brought up with manners, respect, and pure goodness! I had been disciplined whenever I acted up, which was very seldom. I'd had a good spirit that was always full of laughter and love. All my teachers in school had loved me and so had the other kids. I was always at the top of my class with grades and sports. More than anything, I'd always had compassion for the kids who had less talent or were picked on. I'd always stuck up for the kids being bullied and made it a priority to pick the least talented kid first for any game. I was truly full of love. I also enjoyed school until I started high school and began to feel awkward and insecure. My parents were so hardworking that they said if I was going to play hockey, I had to help out with buying the gear, which meant I had to earn a living. Ironically enough, I had always loved business. I had sold hockey cards and set up lemonade stands as early as age three. In eighth grade, I was juggling three paper routes and working at a drugstore stocking shelves on days when I didn't have hockey or other sports.

I was a happy kid with so many dreams for a great life ahead of me, and I was prepared to work as hard as necessary to get it. My backyard was the mountains and a river that contained an abundance of salmon that would run in the summer. I figured out where all the hidden pools were where I could catch one after another. If I wasn't around the house, my parents always knew where to find me. I would catch so many fish that I decided to talk my mom into selling fresh salmon to her clients at a clothing store where she worked. I had three prices for three different sizes of fish that I pulled out of the river. Sometimes I would be down at the river until sunrise, cleaning the fish and then wrapping them up for sales. We had to buy an extra deep freezer just to hold all the fresh fish I was bringing in. That was my first glimpse of making money; I was thirteen years old and bringing in over five hundred dollars a week. I was illegally taking more than my limit from the river, but my mom didn't know the rules, and I could be manipulating with my innocent smile. I was even selling fish to the local Chinese restaurant! The owner loved it because he could get fresh fish for less than half the price he would have to pay wholesale.

As far as trouble goes, I was too busy playing sports to get myself into anything drastic. In high school, my grades slipped because I was trying to find an identity for myself. I was Ryan, the hockey player, but I wanted more. I felt that most of my teachers didn't know as much as they thought or they would be out working in the real world. In my mind, I was going to be signing a big NHL contract, and the last thing I needed was an education from teachers whom I thought didn't care. Of course, there were your exceptions—teachers who really took the time and wanted the best for their students. I always made an effort in their classes and did very well because I never wanted to let down anyone who cared for me. More than anything, I just wanted to use my gifts. I believe every human being on this planet has God-given gifts, and if you don't use your gifts, it's like throwing a piece of your soul away.

At age sixteen, I left home to play junior hockey. My dream was that junior hockey would be an amazing experience and a stepping stone to the heaven of the NHL. But it turned out to be more like a personal hell. While I was full of excitement to take my career to the next level, I was more or less thrown to the wolves. I wasn't prepared for the homesickness I would feel, and I had a hard time adjusting to a new environment where people either loved you or hated you. In school, it had seemed like everyone was my best friend, but in junior hockey at that time, rookie-hazing was in its prime. My first year as a sixteen-year-old boy away from home consisted of being bullied like a dog. I got shoved naked into the bus bathroom with six other guys. Then the veteran players would tape all our clothes tightly together in balls and throw them back into the bathroom, not letting us out until we had all our clothes on, which could take hours. This prank was called "the hot box."

Another time, I was really drunk at an after game party at a hotel on the road. I was playing in the Western Hockey League (WHL) at the time. My dad and brother came to watch. When the team walked into the dressing room, the coach had written an added incentive on the whiteboard. "IF WE WIN TONIGHT, NO CURFEW UNTIL THE BUS LEAVES, AND DRINK AS MUCH AS YOU WANT." The guys on the squad went silently enthusiastic, and we won 6-2. I had promised my dad we would go out to dinner after the game, but instead, I skipped that and got inebriated out of my mind at a downtown bar. When my dad woke me up the next morning, I had been jiffy-marked head-to-toe with toothpaste in my hair. Dad was in shock. My brother Greg was horrified. I slept all the way to the border that next day after taking the ferry back from Vancouver Island.

This kind of hazing was the norm back then. I believe the situation in hockey has improved today, but wow, was I petrified of some of the older players and the coach back then. Fear isn't a great state to be in, and at that age, it really set in for me so that I had little control over my emotions or mastery over self; I was intimidated to say the least. I also stopped becoming a leader. Instead, I did whatever seemed to be cool or necessary to fit in. I became so unhealthy physically and mentally that I would seldom have enough energy to play or practice. Constantly drinking the night before a game didn't help either.

Since I was a young boy, I'd always known that if I wanted something badly enough, nothing could stand in my way; any limitations were self-made prophecies that I made up in my own mind. It was easy—I just had to pursue my dreams with passion and desire! And blessed with amazing talent, I was convinced that hockey was the only career path for me. But injuries and adversities plagued my career, and from the time I was sixteen to twenty, I lived in fourteen different households. Before leaving home that first year, I would lie in bed at night and visualize myself playing alongside and against my idols, whose photographs covered the walls of my room. I wanted to be the best and make my family proud.

For a reason I didn't know then but do now, I was put into situations that made it hard for me to grow as a hockey player and a person. Physically, I was a tall and skinny kid who hadn't been mentally prepared to leave home at such a young age. The day I left home in the summer of 1991, I was filled with enthusiasm while I watched my mom try her best to hold back her tears to no avail. She knew I wasn't mentally ready. Physically, even though I wasn't developed as much as most kids my age, I always used my speed and quick reflexes to avoid impacting hits from much bigger players. My first home was with a single mother and her adopted son. She was a nice enough woman, but the fridge and cupboards were always bare, and I became unhealthy and homesick. I did my best not to complain since my coach played the role of an intimidator, and I didn't want to seem spoiled. From that time on, I only expected failure. You could say my coach tried to motivate me through his intimidations, wanting to toughen me up. Little did I know at that time that the dominating thoughts we feed our subconscious create our reality. I was an emotional kid so when the negatives prevailed, my reality became that which I thought. I became fearful of my coach and teammates and did whatever I could to fit in. In my mind, if hockey wasn't working out the way I intended in the beginning, I could act like the older guys and emulate them off the ice in the party ways.

I started to lose my focus and determination. My grades continued to drop at school. I had attended the local school where I had been playing hockey, but constantly being traded had made it difficult, and hockey had overruled my schooling. In the end, I never would finish high school. I probably got about a grade 10.5 education.

By then, I had developed a bad reputation. I had never intended to hurt anyone; it was just a tender age where finding myself became really difficult. The pattern of my being traded started then; I would always have these high expectations of myself, but something about that first year away from home planted in my mind that I wasn't worthy of great achievements. I stopped believing in myself and was even afraid to go home from fear of being judged by friends and family who had always looked up to me. My skill kept me in the game and I was given many chances. But subconsciously, failure was always in the back of my mind. I thought I didn't deserve success and happiness.

After the trauma of the first few years away from home, I became numb to being traded to different teams and cities.

On the surface, I became a totally different person. The only time I felt I belonged was when I was the life of the party or used my semi-celebrity status to lure in girls for myself and other teammates. I lived a hard and fast party life, and I attracted things into my experience by how I acted and thought. I nearly broke my neck at age seventeen while playing for the Tacoma Rockets in the WHL, Canada's best junior hockey league. I got hit from behind, and before I knew it, the boards were inches away from my chin. I tucked my chin against my chest at the last second, and luckily escaped with a broken shoulder in three places. Depression set in as I watched from the stands for more than three months while players of my caliber were drafted that summer. The following year, I wasn't fully mended and split the '93-94 season between Tacoma and the Regina Pats in Saskatchewan. Right when things were turning around for me, forty-three games into the season, I broke my collarbone in half. That crushed me because, for the first time in three years, I felt part of a team where I was contributing. I self-medicated the intense pain with pain killers and whiskey in the basement of the lady's home where I was living. She was so kind and tried to instill faith and hope in me, but I felt my dreams had been crushed, and my heart at the time had little fight left in it. So knowing that my season was over, I flew home. When my parents picked me up at the airport, I tried my best to put on a happy face and avoid playing the victim role. I had to realize that hockey was a tough game, and it could have been a lot worse. The same year, a friend of mine on another team was paralyzed from the neck down, never to walk again.

The following season, I went back to Regina full of hope, but the coach had it in for me. He had taken an instant dislike to me, having his fun by referring to me in front of the rest of the team as "the rich kid from BC" and asking me, "How much money does your dad send you each week?" He could see by the look on my face how his words made me angry. One day when he asked me, I told him the truth: "Fifty dollars every two weeks." I don't know how much others players' fathers were giving their kids, but my dad, who was actually out of work at the time, was doing his best. It seemed like my comment was just another reason for the coach to have an issue with me. That day, he got really angry at my reply and made me stay after practice; then he pulled me into his office and grabbed me by the throat. I didn't tell my dad about this incident until years later because, knowing my dad, he would have been on the next flight to Regina to set this man straight. Little did my coach know how hard of a time my family was having with me being away, and my dad was doing the best he could to support me unconditionally with whatever means he could. My father was a hardworking man, my role model, and it was only later that my mom told me of his misery and the financial difficulties he underwent to support the family.

I was so scared of my coach and his tactics, but I always put on a happy front. "Fake it until you make it" was my motto, but it was evident I was in a bad place mentally. After having my throat grabbed and being intimidated by my coach, I hated even going to the rink. I was scared, and I was so mentally and physically affected by the incident that it made me sick. Maybe in his twisted way, my coach was trying to scare me into playing better. But more likely, he wanted to bully me, and in the end, he won.

A few days later, I went into the team owner's office and told the owner it was either the coach or me! I felt I needed to make a stand so I told him about some of the coach's unethical behavior toward the guys on our team. I could tell the owner wasn't impressed, but neither was I all that special. Like I said, I had a reputation by that stage of the game. So I quit and went home to play for a team close by.

That might not have been the best idea, however, because all of my friends were close by.

The team was called the Surrey Eagles, and I was living in a mansion where the city mayor and his family lived. The family was never home except for their daughter, who was a few years older than me. She loved that I could party like an animal, and she enjoyed the company I invited over so she could engage in our wild ways. Inside the house was a basketball court and a hot tub on the roof, and there were no real rules. I thought I was untouchable because I had come from a higher league and looked at this opportunity as a free ride. But I lasted only seven games before being traded to a small town in BC called Vernon.

There, I actually had my best junior league experience. For the rest of the year, I played well, and I lived with a great family who made me feel right at home. Having children of their own who were grown up, my hosts treated me like their son. They didn't miss one of my games, and they were always proud to put newspaper clippings of me on the fridge. I was nineteen now, and for the first time in many years, I felt a part of a family away from home. I fit in, and I made some lifelong friends.

But then I got distracted from my primary focus by getting involved with a girl; we had a very toxic relationship—I didn't even know what that meant at the time, but my coaches did, and so did my parents. This girl was beautiful! She was half Native American and lived on the Indian reservation. She had a reputation for being wild, which only attracted me more. I met her at a post-game function at a restaurant, and even though she was there with her boyfriend, we became magnetized to each other. I didn't care that she had a boyfriend, and she clearly had the upper hand in the relationship. I invited both of them back to my house for a dip in the hot tub; in no time, we were getting close in the hot tub. A few days later, I felt I had found my first "true love." I was blinded by her beauty, and she could be nice and act innocent when she was sober. Unfortunately, when she drank, a different side came out, but I thought I could change her. I tried only to see the good in her, but really, I was blinded by toxic love.

Today, I realize that your significant other should bring you higher in life, complement you, and be your best friend. Otherwise, what's the point? I thought that since my parents were still together, couples had to be faithful. A successful relationship requires that you work together as a team. Of course, there are always tests, but true love is unconditional and faithful. People need to remember why they fell for each other in the first place. Sex is biological, but love is spiritual. I had no experience or understanding of these differences yet, so my emotions were sent into toxic overdrive. And when I had no idea how to love myself, how could I love anyone else?

As I finished the year in Vernon, my coaches, teammates, and parents did their best to break up my girlfriend and me. But the more destructive the relationship became, the more I wanted to fix it. So I moved onto the Indian reservation, got a job at the marina pumping gas, and let things explode into mayhem. The next year, I was told by my coaches in Vernon that if I were to play on the team, I would have to break up with her for good and not see her at all. I agreed, but she lured me in again through her sexuality. It would be fair to say I was putty in her hands. When I got caught seeing her at a bar, I was kicked off the team. I was leading the league in scoring at the time, and we were in first place. But she was causing rifts between players and I was allowing her to affect my head. So I was sent packing. Before I even found out I was finished with the team, the newspaper headline read, "Vipers toss Phillips." I was devastated, and my tears and begging my coaches to let me stay were useless.

My assistant coach was a wonderful spirit with a real heart; he got me a spot on the Wichita Thunder, a team in the minor pros. Thank God for him because Wichita is where I met Sadie's mom. Nothing ever happens by mere coincidence. I was jealous and envious—two emotions that need to be avoided at all costs—when I watched my old team win the national championship on television. But I knew I had caused the scene. I actually ran into my old coaches at a local bar a few months later and shook both their hands and congratulated them in utter humility. They deserved their win, and I had been a weak link despite my talents. That's where one bad decision can have a tremendous effect on any individual's destiny. But if not for my kind assistant coach, I wouldn't have had the blessing of Sadie in my life. Therefore, I suggest to my readers that we live in the "cause" of our lives instead of being at the mercy of the effect, which is what happens to most of us who don't set our intentions and live with purpose.

CHAPTER 4
PRISON AND NEW BELIEFS

The next five days of my new life on the "inside" were educational to say the least. I was told that there are state and federal prisons. Because of the amount of product we were apprehended with and that the five of us had been together, each of us would be charged with conspiracy to distribute 100 pounds. I don't know where the extra three pounds went; I guess they just rounded off the number. So for five days, we waited for an answer to whether or not the offense would go to the state or federal court. I met my public defender in the interim; she was a nice, older lady who was very sympathetic to the situation and my family. She looked at me as a young kid who had just made a poor mistake. She also said that Canadians smuggling pot into the United States for large cash profits was part of an all too common trend.

My public defender was almost certain that our case would go to the Feds. And her expertise proved right because on day five we got the verdict that the Feds had picked up the case. Our group was shipped down the I-5 highway in shackles and chains to Seatac Federal Detention Center. Big electric gates opened as our vehicle drove in past armed guards. We had entered a maximum prison, and getting booked in it seemed like being in a bad movie. Although, compared to the Whatcom County dungeon, Seatac was a bit more spacious.

After being booked into Seatac and having our group split up, two of my codefendants and I were led into unit EC, which would be my home for the next eight months. The unit had two levels and consisted of nearly 150 inmates when at full capacity, which was usually the case. A guard was always on duty; he had an office on the ground floor of the unit, referred to as "the bubble," where he would keep a close eye on all the inmates. As soon as I walked into the unit, I saw it was like a zoo! Chants of "New fish" and profanities were shouted by the inmates to intimidate us. I knew I had to stay mentally strong and not break or I would be showing weakness. One of my codefendants and I were led to our cell where we sat on the edge of the bunk bed, shaking our heads in disbelief. It didn't take more than a minute before our cell was full of other Canadians who had committed the same crime. We were told not to trust anyone! The inside was a completely different world that had rules based on respect and seniority. I quickly noticed that the different races there didn't exactly mix, but the Canadians were neutral.

Now began my new life on the inside. I had to accept this reality for what it was or I would lose my mind and go insane. This experience was going to be my biggest test in life so far. I took a look at myself in my cell mirror, which had a horrible reflection. I found it hard to smile at the person looking back at me so I walked away. I didn't look at that mirror much—only on the long days when I needed to see myself say, "Everything's going to be okay!" God knows my sense of humor was partly what was going to get me through the tough days. There was no outside yard, but a smoke pit included a basketball court and ping pong tables. In the common area was a pool table where many fights would take place verbally and physically over unpaid gambling debts. There were three phones the inmates could use to call people in the outside world; every day, I would see so many mixed emotions when men talked to their spouses, kids, or loved ones. It always saddened me to see the tears, usually after the fifteen-minute time limit was over. So many other people had been affected by the actions and mistakes those of us on the inside had made.

Many of us were in for different crimes, so we had been given different penalties for time served. But at the end of the day, we were all alone in there with our thoughts of what our life once was and where it was going. I wasn't accustomed to seeing addicts hooked on heroin be brought in from the street and be forced to suffer massive withdrawals. Later, one of my Mexican friends there told me that when he struggled with withdrawals upon his arrival, the medical staff put him on methadone, a synthetic heroin used to come off the drug. He showed me the track marks on his arms and legs from years of using drugs. I was exposed to so much in there that I'd had no clue about. I was so full of fear, especially the first few months when the prison guards would bombard our unit with dogs to ravage through our cells, rip our beds off the bunks, and search our lockers for drugs or weapons. I heard many stories of hard time done by lifers who had spent more time in prison than in the outside world. In fact, the majority of the prisoners had families who had given up on them.

It may come as a surprise to those who have never been incarcerated, but I met some of the most authentic, genuine souls during my time locked up. I was very blessed to develop a network of friends who really looked out for my wellbeing. And for the first time since I was sixteen, I was sober. My mind was clear and everything that had happened in my life up to this point now made sense.

One person I befriended was a little Japanese man named George (at least, that was his name when they caught him—he had seven aliases). He was in on a conspiracy that involved 250 pounds of marijuana being smuggled over the border in a Canadian army vehicle. I soon learned he had been the mastermind behind the whole operation. He had a family and two kids, but he made it a priority to make me feel at home. He had all the connections in prison with food and other items that were otherwise hard to find. He noticed that I was sleeping all day and didn't want to face reality, so he would come kicking on my door, yelling, "Get the heck up, Phillips, and do your bloody time!" Then he would start laughing. He reminded everyone of a real life Buddha, being short of stature with a large belly.

George would get me up, tell me a few jokes, then lead me to his cell where he would talk about life. George was the first person ever to tell me about the importance of self-love. "Phillips, you got to love yourself!" he would say, and he meant it. I learned so much from him because he actually cared. I could trust him with anything, and I would tell him of my fears. The next thing I knew, he had me writing poetry and reading books. I mean, I was a tough egg to crack. All through high school, I was lucky to get through one book. And poetry? I hadn't written a poem since I was in grade school. The only education I'd had since dropping out of high school I had picked up from life experiences and travel. So you could say that George got into my head. In fact, he told me I would never forget him and his teachings and I haven't. George told me that everything in life is on a frequency; that meant nothing to me at the time; I tried to understand, but I was a work in progress. He would talk about tuning into positive vibrations and that it didn't matter where we were in life at that point. It was about focusing on the positive aspects of life and using my current life lesson as a building block to an amazing future full of unlimited possibilities that I could create with my mind.

Soon, I started writing every day. We would write together, picking a topic (such as "mountains") and the next day compare what we had written. George became like a father figure to me in prison, and his words and thoughts started to give me a deep understanding of how the universe works as a whole. He reminded me every day, and showed me through his personality and words, that just because we were prisoners in a institution didn't mean we had to be prisoners in our minds.

It wasn't long before I started to spend hours every day visualizing a brighter future for myself once this experience was over. I started writing positive affirmations in a journal; I would lie on my bunk, listen to music, and block out the inside world I was trapped in, taking my mind onto sandy beaches and faraway lands that penetrated the walls holding me prisoner. I learned that I came from a source of love, and that I could block out any form of negativity I chose. I expressed thanks every time I opened my eyes to a new day and quickly began to realize that my overall perspective of life was changing dramatically. All the guards started to treat me differently, and my cell attracted all sorts of people from different races where we would talk about family and how blessed we all were to be alive on this planet no matter what had happened in the past. George became a sort of life coach to me, and what he taught me, I then taught to others there who were searching for inner peace in a place run on anxiety and fear of the unknown.

I kept busy in prison! I refused to waste my time. I was one of the only white folks who would play basketball after dinner on a nightly basis, and by doing so, I formed an amazing bond with a lot of African Americans who embraced me due to my open mind and heart. I would walk for many miles a day around the unit. I also made it my mission to reach out to the Mexicans, who all stuck together, and in no time, they were bringing me homemade jail burritos. It was one big game in there now for me, but it was the game of life and the reality that love given to all was the eternal elixir of life. I was giving and receiving love and being rewarded with friendships and a safety valve of security. The so-called tough guys would come to me with their problems, and I would always find a way to inject faith into their minds through being completely honest and open. I came to realize I was there for a reason.

I had six different cell mates during my time in EC. I shared many different emotions of happiness and sadness with them. When my parents came to visit me, they were proud to hear the guards tell them I was a goodhearted man. That made me feel good because the guards felt I wasn't a threat, and they understood that my purpose in there was to give hope to others. That was my first true experience of rendering useful service without expecting any wages or compensation in return. In prison, we were all equal. There were no fancy cars or nice houses. People might brag about what they had on the outside, but on the inside, all we had was who we truly were as human beings.

The hardest part of being in EC was when the guards would come into the unit for a surprise visit called a "shakedown." At least ten guards would come and ravage through our cells. They would empty all the contents of our lockers on the floor and search for drugs and weapons. This search felt so violating. I never had anything to hide, but others did. The guards would throw all 150 or so of us inmates into the smoke pit while we waited for them to do their job. Then when it was over, we would have to put our beds back together and clean up our lockers. When I was in the smoke pit, I could see the sadness, the anger, and the sense of defeat in the men with whom I shared the unit.

Another difficult part of my imprisonment was that we were right by the airport, so I would sit on my bunk for hours watching planes come and go, wondering where their destinations were and wishing I had the freedom to go wherever I wanted like the people on those planes. I thought of family and love and how I was missing out on so much in life. Because I don't judge people any longer, I can humbly say to every man or woman, that while crime can pay financially, even if you have all the money in the world, it's only temporary. My heart goes out to every family with a son, daughter, or other family member who made the decision to break the law, then had to pay the price of jail, death, or a substance abuse problem. I met plenty of nice guys while involved in the drug business, but now many of them are no longer on the planet. "What made me any different from them?" I often wondered. "With all the abuse and close calls, why am I still alive?" The answer came many years later after more self-inflicted misery. A power greater than myself let me get away with enough to realize that it was do or die!

When my day of sentencing finally arrived, I received the minimum mandatory sentence of eighteen months. All the time I had spent in EC was time served, and if I was a good boy, I would get another month and a half off for "good behavior," providing I didn't get into any fights or abuse drugs—drugs and alcohol were readily available in the institution. Visitors would hide drugs in small bags in their mouths and make the transfer from civilian to inmate. The guards, I'm sure, were keen to this, but they knew that they could not stop everything. New prisoners who had just come off the street would conceal drugs in places I'd rather not say, and then they would profit off them by trading drugs for food or other items. I just minded my manners and took everything one day at a time. I got into the routine of doing push-ups and of filling garbage bags with water, putting a shirt over the top of the bag, and using a broomstick to go through the shirt to serve as a curl bar or shoulder press. As difficult as prison was, I created a better life for myself in there. I had respect from everyone because I treated others with kindness. How could I be bitter about a situation I had created for myself? So the days turned into weeks and the weeks turned into months. At first, it had seemed like my sentence would take forever to complete, but I crossed off every day on the calendar in my locker until my release date of January 2, 2002 approached. I would have to spend my second Christmas and New Year's away from loved ones, but the time was nearing its end.

I could write a full book on my experiences of prison, but I intend for this book to be a story about happiness and positive change in the world. To borrow an expression from Napoleon Hill, "Every Adversity, every setback carries with it the seed of an equal or greater advantage." When only two weeks remained to my sentence, time seemed to stand still. Fear started to set in; in many ways, I'd become institutionalized and accustomed to the ways on the inside. I knew that on January 2nd, I would be transferred to Immigration and Naturalization Services for at least a week before they released me back to my home country of Canada. My goodbyes were kept short as I took one last glance at what had been my home for the past sixteen-and-a-half months. I was led down an elevator and put into a waiting room for a few hours before being put into shackles and chains for the last time. I was then led into a big white van and taken to INS where I felt fresh air for the first time in over five hundred days. It felt amazing as the sun beamed down on my pale face. You never realize how blessed you are until what you have is taken away from you; temporarily losing my freedom had taught me how sacred freedom is.

I was in a cell at INS with all walks of life. I was one of the only English speaking people in my large cell, which had twenty inmates also awaiting their release. But the end was near. After nine days in INS, my name was called. I was in a simultaneous state of joy, shock, and gratitude. I had made it! I had done my time and learned a lot, although what I was to gain through this experience wouldn't really hit me until many years later.

I now was led into an old elevator down to the first floor of the INS building and put into a small holding cell with the rest of the guys who were involved in the conspiracy. I couldn't help being exhilarated and feeling full of happiness that I was going home. I was being a bit loud, making jokes with the people I knew until one of the guards decided he didn't like my sense of humor. He told me "If you don't shut up, you will be missing your ride back to Canada," so I didn't say another word until our group was loaded into a big white van and we were at least ten minutes down the interstate. What had seemed like an eternity now felt like a short dream. As I stared out the window, I thought about all the people I had met in prison who still had a long road ahead of them before they would also know freedom. It was my first sight of the outside world in some time, and I felt so overcome with emotion that I was speechless. The ride to the border was about two-and-a-half hours, but it seemed like twice that long.

When we arrived, the doors were opened by the officers, and I stepped into the cold night of January 11th and my freedom. When I said a sincere goodbye and thanked the officers for the ride, one of them said, "See you again soon" in a very sarcastic tone, insinuating that I would break the law again and end up back inside. When I walked into the Canadian customs at the border, the customs officers welcomed me and my group home with smiles and open arms. They could tell we had been through a lot emotionally and physically. I told them, "You have no idea how happy I am to see you guys." My identification had been sent to the border by my parents. I picked it up and was free to go back into Canada. The second I left the building, I jumped into the air and screamed at the top of my lungs in elation and utter joy that I was a free man! For that brief time, I was one of the happiest guys in the world. I didn't know what to do with myself! I felt reborn!

One of the guys released with me had his girlfriend pick him up, so I jumped into the car with them and got a ride into my hometown of North Vancouver. His girlfriend had twelve cold Coronas that we dove into immediately. It was the first time I'd had alcohol in my system for some time, so it wasn't long before I caught a buzz. I decided not to let my parents know I was home that night since I wanted to celebrate with one of my best friends who had been there for me throughout my entire stint with weekly uplifting letters. He had kept my faith alive that I had people who truly cared for me beyond just my immediate family.

Upon arriving at my friend's house, I became a chatterbox! I didn't know what to do with myself. He insisted I take a shower. That must have been the longest shower of my life! And out of nowhere, my mind went back to my old habits before my life in prison. My friend also had new clothes waiting for me. I had forgotten what it was like to dress like a normal person because I'd become so used to prison gear. It wasn't until a few weeks later as I regained my health that my friend told me I had looked like I'd just gotten out of a concentration camp when he first saw me.

My pal made a call for some cocaine so we got high! Then he asked me what I wanted to do, but I didn't really know what to say. He said, "Let's go for a steak." My appetite wasn't really there after a few lines of blow, but we went to the Cactus Club, a local hot spot where attractive girls served. It been a long while since I'd had any contact with a woman, so my once confident charm around the ladies was gone. I couldn't even look these girls in the eye. And when it came time to order my food, I clammed up and just said, "I'll have what he's having." It felt odd that someone was serving me after months of having specific rules and times for meals that were never satisfying unless George made one of his famous soups from good food brought up from his kitchen connection.

That night, I got smashed drunk at a club down on the water of the North Shore. I saw many old friends, and after putting back who knows how many, I was hugging everyone in sight. I got a lot of love that night from people who knew what had happened. All kinds of rumors had spread around town after I went down. One rumor was that I had attacked the judge after she sentenced me to ten years. Funny how people love to talk and bend the truth. But I was out now, and it felt like I had all the tools to create a new life based on a lot of the principles of self-discipline and faith that I had learned behind those walls and in my jail cell. Still, old habits die hard and turning my life around on the outside would be a difficult process as I would quickly learn.

CHAPTER 5
INCEPTION OF *RETURN TO HAPPINESS*

Seeing my parents for the first time outside the visiting room at the prison felt wonderful. It was awkward at first, as if they really didn't know how to treat me. But as usual, they showered me with unconditional love. They recommended that I see a shrink because they had heard about how hard it is to adjust back to the real world after being institutionalized. But being a stubborn individual, I refused any help from outside sources. I closed off all my emotions and pretended like nothing was wrong. I hid all the hurt that was inside me, including the emotional baggage of missing my daughter, and throwing my hockey career down the drain through poor decisions. My awakening process was going to be slow and gradual because I hadn't yet learned the art of letting the past go so I could live in the present moment, even though I'd had a sense of that need from the time I was a child.

I remember clear as day one time when I was eleven and my mom was driving me to a hockey game. I told my mom,

"You know, Mom, we are the creators of our own reality!" She looked at me and wondered where I was coming from.

As a young boy, I was always fascinated with the universe, the planets, and the stars. I used to ask my mom questions like: "If you keep going up into the sky forever, where does it end?" I was always intrigued with nature, and while growing up, I'd had a forest for my backyard playground. I always felt at one and at peace when I was away from the city and in the mountains or on the water fishing. Now after all these years, I realized that everything in the visible world is derived from nature. Human beings are part of nature, being created out of the formless and brought forth into the world of thought and forms.

But upon my release from prison, despite all I had learned, I did not know what my purpose should be. My awakening would come, but it would take time. I didn't become a "good boy" overnight. It's funny how many of us in this world have to suffer all kinds of emotional and physical pain before the light turns on inside our minds and wakes us up to our true nature and the unlimited power we hold inside ourselves. In 2005, three years after my release from prison, I was still on a dark path; I was drinking and using drugs at least four days a week. On the surface, it looked like I was living the dream...but when the party was over, I felt empty, lost, and scared. I was portraying an image that wasn't me. I was drifting through life, still making poor choices that didn't align with who I truly was. I was nice to most people, but I couldn't find that inner peace. I firmly believe we are creatures of habit and that we take on the traits of the people with whom we associate, and that's what was happening to me.

I had by now gone from being a bar star to a reclusive partier at my downtown condo where I would binge for days on end. It would start out with booze and then mad amounts of cocaine to the point where every time I did it, I would think I was dying! I would ask whoever was with me to "Check my pulse! Am I dying?" Now years later, I realize my inner soul is what had been dying while trying to tell me to stop before I lost my life. One morning, after a three-day alcohol and drug binge with a friend, I woke up and staggered into the shower, unable to look at myself in the mirror. When I got out of the shower, I did look in the mirror and saw death! The party was over.

The following day, a friend called AA for us and we went to our first meeting. It felt good to be at the meeting, but my ego was still in the way. I wasn't a very good listener, and the words I heard didn't sink in completely. I thought I was just an extreme guy! No matter what I did in life, it had to be to the extreme. I was a binger, and I ingested whatever was put in front of me once I had enough alcohol in me. I partied with lots of coke dealers, so the drugs were always free. Ecstasy came into the mix all too often, and there would be nights where I would lose track of how many pills I had taken. That I am still alive and made it out of the darkness into the light is a miracle.

After a few months of going to AA meetings, my life started to get better. I broke up with my girlfriend because it was a toxic relationship. I also got my first small glimpse of spirituality. I was experiencing firsthand how in most cases when we eat healthy foods and treat our bodies well, nature will do the rest and reward us with a renewed spirit. There are always your exceptions—such as when people suffer from diseases and accidents—but if we are alive on this physical plane called earth, then everyday it's up to us how we treat ourselves. All things in moderation. However, temptation can make a fool out of us all, so after nearly three months of sobriety, I found myself at a bar doing shots and slamming back as many beers as I could before closing time. Back into the world of partying I went.

Then I met a girl I had a crush on but hadn't seen in months. Sobriety had affected me in a very positive way. I looked healthy and younger; I had lost twenty pounds I had gained from booze and a poor diet. She said, "Ryan, you look great; you're not an alcoholic." Then she kissed me as she jumped into my arms. And just like that, I was drunk again. Learning the hard way became a blueprint pattern, but God knows I wanted to crack the code.

Let's talk about close calls. For some time after my release, I didn't lead an honest life. When I first got out, I had all these plans to become an actor. I loved entertainment. I thought I had some talent in that field, and I definitely knew I could play a lot of characters—God knows I'd been one enough times in my life. I could play the athlete, the gangster, the lover—you get my drift. I always loved doing impressions and making stories with my creative side. But I chose to associate myself with people on a different path. Still, it was all for a reason because it led me to where I am today. A few times, I was extorted. One time in particular, I was accused of stealing 70 kilos of cocaine. The people who either made up this lie or thought it was true did not play games. I was called to a meeting in an Asian restaurant in a rough area of town. When I drove by the place, all the lights were off and bars were in the windows. When I saw that, my heart started to race. I knew something was terribly wrong. I had never sold coke! It wasn't my business, but my name had been blackened by a guy in Los Angeles. Later, I told the man on the phone that I didn't feel safe going into that place, and if he wanted to meet me, he could come to a busy public restaurant downtown where we could talk and work out this misunderstanding. My hands were sweaty as I waited with six of my friends at the restaurant. You always know when something isn't right. Right, it wasn't! Thirty-plus thugs rolled into the place and surrounded my table. I was then told that I owed them two million dollars by noon the next day...or else.

I was shaking like a leaf, and every time I tried to talk, they would cut me off. Still, if I had gone to that restaurant,

I don't think I would be writing these lines. Later, a friend in Los Angeles told me he had heard through the grapevine who had accused me. I was given the culprit's name and told there were hundreds of pages on the Internet about this guy, who was a major con artist. I looked him up later that evening after I happened to see his face on an episode of *NBC Dateline*. I had to pay for my name to get cleared along with that of my partner. And I had to take a lie detector test the very next day as well, which I passed with flying colors. That was enough to wake me up. I didn't sleep for a few days because I was so scared for my life.

Some time later, I was asked to party with the guys who had helped to bail me out. It just so happened that they were friends with one of the guys who was at the restaurant that day. I was having drinks with him when he said he was the one who was going to put a gun to my head and put me in a trunk. Now we were buddies, and he told me, "You're a nice guy." After that, my name was out there and I had gangs asking me to join them; they had all heard exaggerated stories of what had happened. I became so fearful that I told my girlfriend to pack her bags and we flew to Costa Rica to hide out for a few months.

I had lost everything at this point. Even just finding the will to live was hard. On the plane ride to Costa Rica, I started reading two books that gave me some hope and knowledge that I had always known deep down. The books were Eckhart Tolle's *The Power of Now* and Rhonda Byrne's *The Secret.* I hadn't read a book during all my brief high school years, but now I was willing to try anything to make myself feel better. My girlfriend read *The Secret* from front to back on the ride there. I then picked it up and read what the "Law of Attraction" meant. (That which is like unto itself is drawn to it.) Then like a light switch going off in my mind, I was able to make sense of my whole life experience. *The Power of Now* brought into my awareness the power of the present moment and how everything we create is created in the present! I began to ask people, "What time is it?" They would look at me like I was crazy because they saw I was wearing a watch. Then I would reply "RIGHT NOW!"

I became a total bookworm. I started blowing through books, but spiritual books intrigued me the most. I was also blessed to watch a YouTube video of Bob Proctor, in which he spoke about how he had overcome poverty and adversity forty years earlier. Someone close to him had given him Napoleon Hill's book *Think and Grow Rich*, which had changed his life and skyrocketed him to success. Right away, I purchased the book.

The moment I started reading *Think and Grow Rich*, my body was covered in goose bumps! I could feel the message's connection to my inner being, my spirit. The book made so much sense that I could actually visualize and hear Napoleon talking to me. In the book, one major statement Napoleon makes is, "Whatever the mind conceives and believes, the mind can achieve." As I began studying the book and using its principles, my whole world started to change just like promised. Napoleon Hill inspired me! I have so much gratitude in my heart for Mr. Proctor and Mr. Hill for somehow guiding me to that book that I can't sum it up in words. Everything I would do in my life from that point on I knew would be based on the principles I learned in that book, and then I would expand on them with my knowledge gained to give back to humanity whatever good I could.

I started looking at everything from a different vantage point! I came to the point where being so consciously aware began to frighten me. I could see energy or colorful auras surrounding people. I would say to my family "We are electricity" or "We are vibrating" and "Who you see in front of the mirror and your name isn't who you are." They thought I had lost my mind. I wanted everyone to see and feel what I was experiencing. I was actually channeling nonphysical energy most of the time now. I always knew why I felt good or bad, and how I could quickly change my vibration.

A few more close calls came knocking on my door soon after I got home from Thailand. A friend of mine had lost some money in a transaction gone sour, so I went with him to try to help him get it back. It wasn't a great idea to meet at a food court close to closing time with people you have never met. In minutes, we were surrounded and my friend was told to back down. I could see very well that these people meant business. Even though it was a rip off, they had made it right in their heads. Last I heard, a few people who were there that night are no longer living. I look back at that situation now and thank God I walked out of there alive. I find it hard at times to think back to some of the situations I put myself in out of choice. Always a people pleaser, I found that, for the most part, that dangerous game always worked against me. I now know why I suffer from post-traumatic stress from the business—it has made me feel a duty to give sound advice to youth who are lost and on the brink of making decisions that could cost them their lives. I know I can't hold on to the past, but I jump at any opportunity I have to give youth or even people my age or older advice that could help them.

By the time I started the *Return to Happiness* project a few years ago, I was far removed from anything remotely close to the nature of organized crime, but some people don't believe others can change. At one time, these people had been "friends" of mine; they had heard that I was still moving and shaking when instead I was doing my best to give to others and make a positive change in the world. When I heard that they wanted to extort me for a large sum of money, it made me sick to my stomach, and for a brief minute, I thought about throwing in the towel on *Return to Happiness*. I thought, "How in God's name can someone want to harm me? I haven't done anything to these people." But I had to see it from the bigger picture—people talk and stories get distorted, so they had heard I was still in the game. They knew I didn't have any muscle behind me at this point because at one time they had been my muscle! When I first heard about this situation, I didn't know what to do; the easy way out would have been to go to the police, but I always felt that in the end, they would reap what they sowed and it would be taken care of for me. As hard as it was at times, I just sent them love through my heart. The funny thing about the situation is that it wasn't just one person—it was two men, plus whoever they had following them. If they had been men of integrity, they would have approached the situation differently, but as the old saying goes, gang violence and extortion is never a one man game; it's gang or mob mentality.

It may seem farfetched and unbelievable to some, but at this point, I heard this inner voice that I like to refer to as my Higher Self. The message my Higher Self gave me was crystal clear: "Leave Vancouver at once and show the world happiness in whatever shape or form." I did leave Vancouver and used this situation as my motivation. Let me tell you, not a day goes by that I don't think about how my safety was at risk. Before I left, I came clean to my family about everything I had done in the past. I couldn't be dishonest if I tried. My family was full of fear as well. And, of course, word got around the gossip mill that I owed a bunch of money for protection fees and some other nonsense that was so far from the truth and what I now stood for. I used to think it was cool that these guys had my back. I had felt untouchable with them as friends. But once the moneymaking stopped, they were no longer friends. And these guys didn't play nice. I gave the names of these two angry people to all my family members and friends and told them that if anything ever happened to me, these men would most likely be the cause since I had no other enemies I could recollect. Meanwhile, I continued to pray for them, instead of wishing them harm. I prayed that they would just move on and come to grips with reality like I was doing.

Something inside of me had now changed and I believed, "It's my responsibility to have a purpose and do something with my life." The starting point for me was that I could use all my adversities and failures, which had only been tests, to help others! Since my release from prison, I had tried to make a living selling screen doors, helping my dad paint houses, in real estate, and through many other avenues. I had even tried to make a hockey comeback in 2009 in Slovakia, but the language barrier was a big hurdle and made me give closure to my hockey life. It was time to let go of all my past if I were to succeed in the present and future.

I decided to buy a Sony XDCAM to shoot film because I loved to travel and experience other cultures. My new dream was to host a travel show. I had these big plans of showing the world in all its beauty, immersing myself with the locals wherever I was, and at the same time, showing that I was having an all around awesome time while doing it. Then I ran into an old friend on the seawall in Vancouver. He had a reputation for being a wild one, but I had a soft spot for him, especially when he told me how he was changing his life by focusing on the positive. He had just finished a landmark education course and seemed to be on track in changing his life. When I told him about my desire to film a travel show, he wanted to jump onboard.

We flew to Thailand a few weeks later and started filming. I named the show *Spin the Globe.* I loved being in front of the camera, and having the opportunity to learn as I went along was a really cool experience. But *Spin the Globe* wasn't meant to be. The cameraman we found did his best, but we were rookies at the game. We weren't organized like we should have been. We got some great shots, but at the end of the day, it was like a mixture between *Jackass: The Movie* and a home travel video.

But no way was I going to give up on my dream. I had

come too far in the past few years to stop believing in myself, and giving up was never an option. I just had to plan things out better. So the same friend and I decided to fly to Spain with a more experienced cameraman and a plan. This time, I was a lot more focused and at ease in front of the camera. I was having fun now and new ideas were daily popping into my head for how we could make "The best travel show ever!" That became all my buddy and I talked about. I knew we had something good. I wanted the show to reflect the importance of giving back to people in need, as well as include lots of reasons for laughter and some off-the-wall personality. I would be the witty one who would egg on my friend to do insane things (like fight a bull); then we would show up in a poor neighborhood to give soccer jerseys to kids. Unfortunately, the show never manifested into reality. The good heart intention was there, but something just didn't jive. We got a good trailer out of the deal and some great footage, but the show just didn't resonate with what I believed in and my buddy moved on to other things.

I decided to take some time for myself and really focus on what I wanted in my life after that experience. More than anything, I wanted to give the world something amazing that would inspire people to believe in themselves. I wanted people to know that no matter what had happened in the past, we all have the ability to change our current situation through the power of focused thought and giving back to others. I was now living my life mainly in the nonphysical dimension, not concentrating on material things, but by reading spiritual books and seeing the world from their perspective. I began looking at people differently. I saw them as vessels through which a Higher Power was channeled. I began manifesting things at a rapid speed, but not everything I manifested was good.

For a time, I became scared of my thoughts. I thought perhaps people wanted to kill me or kidnap me. People tried extorting me for things I no longer did. My intuition again told me I had to leave Vancouver or something bad was going to happen. But I stuck to my dream to give as much happiness to others as I could while teaching what we can all do if we harness the power of our minds and direct that power to what is good and truthful in life. I lost all willingness to hate, and I could no longer get angry or jealous. I no longer desired a stupid amount of riches. I longed for realness in my life. I wanted to be with people who loved me for me. I thought maybe I could set a trend that it's cool to be you. To make others realize that each and every human being is a perfect blessing. We are the people who let the negatives in. We are the ones who choose to hate, so it's up to us either to change for the better or to continue to create misery in the world. Standing for what is good is sacred. Since we're here, why can't we make every life experience worthwhile? Yes, not everything is great at all times, but it's all happening in a divine order, so why shouldn't it be great? I knew that giving your own happiness in abundance creates a pattern. That's when I came up with the idea and name for *Return to Happiness*.

I started the project by getting a website up and running, and I started writing blogs and doing short videos about how I was doing my very best to help others improve their lives. I told how I had been down and out mentally and emotionally, and how I had fought back against all the negatives in my life to create a better life for myself through rendering useful service to others. Yes, I had studied many self-help books and religions, but *Return to Happiness* wasn't about that. It was about leading a happier life, and everyone was welcome to be a part of the alliance. All the people along my journey in life had helped me to discover myself, and all the people in the world were the people to whom I wanted to give back my heart and happiness. I knew I was not a guru or a self-help preacher. But I had been through enough experiences in my life that I knew I could help others who were going through similar struggles. I knew I could give hope to people! And that was now my mission!

At this time, I made contact with Khalil, a cameraman from Belgium who was living in Montreal. I went to visit him to discuss the project. We met in a hotel room downtown and talked for hours. I figured we could create a documentary about my concept of filming a travel show. I would highlight the beauty of a country, immerse myself in the communities, have a blast and make people laugh, and most importantly, wherever we traveled, I would give back to some sort of cause or a family in need. I wanted to show the full package of life with teaching aspects and the interconnectedness that we all share globally as human beings. I didn't need a co-host; I wanted to do it my way and attract as much happiness along the journey through setting my sails of thought into such positive vibrations that the film would just write itself and create a story.

Khalil and I clicked immediately because, as different as we were, we shared a lot of the same views on life. Most importantly, I respected how he spoke of his family. We went for some Lebanese food after walking the freezing streets of Montreal. We came to the agreement that we were going to film the best travel documentary ever made by two men. I mean, why not shoot for the stars and aim high. We were both getting really juiced and inspired. Our thoughts were feeding off each other, and we were frantically jotting down one idea after the next. I was ready to lay everything on the line for this project and so was he. I wish to this day we had filmed that entire conversation because the majority of people would have thought we were crazy from how excited we were. But our sole purpose was to make an impact on the world and give our viewers something worth watching that would open their hearts and minds.

After I flew back to Vancouver, I began daily to write down ideas and figure out how our journey should start. I wasn't some famous actor who had taken classes on how to be in front of the camera, but I knew one thing—I could be my authentic self! I wanted to prove to all the people in the world what a blessing it is that there's only one you—how special that one you really is, and how wonderful it is that you can never be duplicated. I knew I could be me and that counted for a lot because I had done so much inner work over many years. All the ups and downs and close calls I'd had in life would make me genuine and provide the perfect platform to connect to people who have been through any kind of trauma. I wanted to give the film's viewers an action-packed adventure with no ego.

What inspired me more than anything was the love I had in my heart for my daughter. I wanted to show her what kind of father I was since we had been separated for so many years, except for summer visits and one Christmas in 2007. Otherwise, the telephone and Skype were our only means of communication. Thank God that Sadie's mother and I had a good relationship. Her mom was now proud of me for making serious life changes. For years I had judged others, which in turn was just a mirror reflection of judging myself. Now I had to learn to quit being hard on others and myself. My physical body was overweight and totally out of tune from when I was playing sports as a kid. So if I were to make a complete transformation, I had to concentrate on health as well. My desire to be a role model to others wasn't going to be half-assed. Next, I had to forgive all the people I thought had wronged me in the past and let go of all resentments. I had to see my part in the actions I played to allow these people and events to affect me in my current experience. Whenever I thought a negative thought from the past and brought that feeling into my present vibration, it would hinder my growth, so I had to learn to live in the present. I wanted so badly now to go in the right direction.

I had always loved people! People from all races and creeds had intrigued me since I was a boy. Now as I eliminated forms of jealousy, selfishness, cynicism, greed, and anger, I began to love humanity as a whole on such a higher level than before. I started to see people's inner beings as an energy system of their vibrations. I felt their vibrations on a very deep level. I'm not an advocate of telling people how to live and run their lives. I only can tell them how when I decided to stop poisoning my body and mind with substances, my whole inner and outer world changed. I began to see how cause and effect run the universe. The Law of Attraction was actually in some sense the Law of Vibration. It may sound off the wall, but I could actually see things vibrating. And when the physical manifestation of what I was thinking always made its way swiftly into my experience, I knew I was walking the line of a beautiful spiritual experience. In my heart and soul, I began to love everyone. We all come from love, and in essence, I was returning to my true nature.

Khalil came to Vancouver at the end of the first week of January, 2012. That first day of filming, my intuition told me to take the two-hour drive from my parents' house to the base of the logging road where all my legal troubles had started. It was beautiful out, although very cold with snow on the ground. I explained to the camera how everything went down the day of my arrest. From the time he had arrived in Vancouver, Khalil had wanted that camera on as much as possible. "The Big Belgium Beauty," as I would I end up calling him, wanted to know whom he had gotten into bed with on our endeavor by filming everything about me. This young twenty-six-year-old DJ/cameraman was filming a reformed criminal and alcoholic whose biggest dream was to help change the world through positive love and giving. Go figure—some people can't grasp the fact that people can change, but Khalil was trying to understand and believe it.

After that first take on camera, I looked at my phone and saw that the date was January 11th. "My God," I said as a lump formed in my throat and my eyes swelled up. It was ten years to the day of my release, and we were filming the beginning of *Return to Happiness*! "What a blessing," I thought, as I remembered back to the exact moment where I was ten years ago to the day.

No matter where this film was going, it just felt right. I was doing something I believed in. I had a plan, and nothing would stand in my way. More than anything, I had created a purpose for myself. I knew what I wanted and the future was up to Khalil and me and whoever else came across our path to help us create it.

Southeast Asia has long held a special place in my heart; it's where I've experienced much inner peace. So I decided that sacred land would be the perfect platform for a happiness adventure. I'll never forget my first trip over there in 2005 with a friend. After spending less than twenty-four hours insanely partying in Bangkok with no sleep, we were able to get an early flight to the island of Phuket. When we arrived, he went and crashed in the hotel room close to the beach. I couldn't sleep; something drew me to the Andaman Sea. I wandered down to the beach alone and saw a lot of people weeping and mourning the loss of loved ones. I realized it was one year to the day that the massive tsunami had rocked thirteen different countries, including Thailand. Doves were being released, and flowers were being thrown into the sea. This event hit close to home because one of my good friends, Chris, had lost both his mother and father in the disaster in a town about two hours away called Khao Lak. I said some prayers and thought about all the loved ones and families who had been affected by this event. I looked up into the sky and gave thanks for my own life and then made my way back to the hotel.

Despite this tragedy, whenever I would see Chris around, he was always very positive. He now had a family of his own, and I learned that his family had built a school for the orphaned children of Khao Lak in memory of his parents. I decided that school would be the first stop on our journey! When I saw Chris a few days before my adventure in Southeast Asia would begin, he told me how he had formed a strong bond with these kids, who had lost so much, and how they were always so happy and loving when a caring adult was present. He told me how full of life they were, and how he had literally become a human jungle gym to them when he visited. Now I would be meeting these kids in the near future.

Before Khalil and I embarked on our journey to Southeast Asia, I also met with an intuitive healer named Helen. I have always believed that a special power governs all things in this universe so I was open to what this kind woman had to say. I'm a firm believer that we all create our own reality in life, but I also believe that people who are in tune and highly sensitive to energies can pick up on our vibrations and forecast some future events. "What the heck! Just maybe she has some insight on our trip," I thought. What started off as visit full of laughs soon became serious and emotional. Helen said she saw us making a documentary film that would be shown in various film festivals in the United States. I got emotional when she said that since I wasn't allowed across the U.S. border and dearly wanted to visit Sadie there.

Helen then proceeded to tell me that she saw me "surrounded by kids, because so many in the world are so ill-treated," and that I could bring them some happiness. I told her "That is my dream" and "Sadie is one of the main driving forces behind the film." She sincerely told me that Khalil and I were about to find ourselves in many ways through the filming of this movie. We had told her nothing of our plans, but soon we would see that she had been right.

Khalil flew back to Montreal for a week or so while I kept setting my intentions daily and affirming to myself that *Return to Happiness* would help people and bring more hope into their lives. I was consumed by the project and every fiber of my being radiated with love and happiness. I put out so many positive vibrations into this upcoming adventure because I knew that we radiate and attract that which we are.

Our date of departure was Saturday, January 26, 2012. The Friday before, I got a call from the Department of Homeland Security stating that I had to come in on Tuesday to sign some papers at the airport for a waiver I had applied for over a year earlier for possible readmission to the United States. This call came as a shock to me since I had been applying for many years, and now what I wanted seemed impossible because I was leaving the following day. The gentleman on the phone was so nice, and he told me that the Department of Homeland Security was seriously considering my readmission. I told him of my film project about positive change in the world and how I couldn't change my ticket. He said he would check with his advisor and get back to me within ten minutes. I was anxiety-ridden while I awaited his call. But when the nice man called back, he said they were making a first exception and that if I could come in early the next day, he would do his best to take my fingerprints and run the waiver through to the decision-makers in D.C. I thanked him from the bottom of my heart. My dad took me to the airport the next morning where I was passed through heavy security and then entered an office where I was fingerprinted and I signed off on some documents.

I told the officer the purpose of my trip to Southeast Asia, how much family meant to me, and how that one mistake had taught me so much about this life we live. He loved the whole concept of *Return to Happiness*, but his exact words were "I can't even believe that they are considering letting you back into the USA, but I'm really pulling for you." I attached to the documentation a link to my website about how I was trying to help others through my setbacks.

I hoped that information might have an impact on the decision maker. It warmed my heart to know this trip was starting with some good karma.

I stayed at the airport hotel while anxiously waiting for Khalil. When his flight was due, I ran down to the Domestic Canadian arrivals and greeted Khalil with a big hug. He had a huge grin on his face. He had never been to Southeast Asia, so I told him how magical it was over there, about the people, their smiles, and the beauty of the landscape and the sunsets. I was ultra-excited. We had both put relationships with significant others aside to tackle a project we really believed in. As a result, we would both eventually break up with our girlfriends. Some resentment was felt by both the women in our lives at that time, and we couldn't blame them, but I couldn't take on that emotion. Instead, I had to concentrate my energy on all the good that was now to come.

Khalil and I chilled in the room for a few hours. He spilled out all the camera gear and started taking pictures like a camera junkie. I was laughing silently inside because I knew he was in for a serious eye-opener once we touched down in Asia. We went around the airport and started filming. The one question we asked hundreds of people in the airport was, "What makes you happy in life?" We got so many different answers: love, sex, family, kids, pets, money…. It was always cool to get a different perspective on happiness. Most people at the airport were happy, of course, because they were taking off on a trip.

Since we were leaving late that night, my parents came to have dinner with us and say their goodbyes. During dinner, we all had a great talk about life. My dad gave us some added inspiration by telling us, "Just live and smile every day; be grateful and love every moment." That meant a lot coming from him since he had battled his own adversity a few years earlier with heart surgery. He had made it, though, and since then, he has lived his life like a warrior. He gives back to many causes and is always there to lend a hand and be a friend to someone in need. My mom is also very strong. Rarely is she in a poor mood, and our relationship has been a dream since I wised up and chose a different path. Our goodbyes that day were a tad emotional. We were used to goodbyes since I had been leaving home since sixteen, but in the eyes of my parents, I was still their baby boy. We hugged it out, and then they took off, honking the horn.

I felt I had now found the seed in my negative experiences that would bring me greater benefits, and if I kept planting more seeds, the benefits and blessings from it would be never-ending; planting those seeds was exactly what I intended to do now that I knew how the process worked. And while I might never come to welcome adversity in my life, I had learned to deal with it in a completely different way—through self-control and gratitude when things weren't going as I intended. Adversity builds character!

We didn't have a lot of time to get through security now, and Khalil wanted to get some shots at the airport. I was getting mentally prepared for the long flight while staying focused on the mission. I could feel this trip was the start of something very special. This was the story of *Return to Happiness*.

CHAPTER 6
BANGKOK—THE JOURNEY BEGINS

The long flight to Bangkok wasn't all bad, even though I've had a phobia of flying since my youth. We had a quick layover in Hong Kong, so we ripped into the city for a few hours. It was the Chinese New Year. The city was pretty dead since the New Year's celebrations the night before must have exhausted a lot of people. A big red bus pulled up to us on the street and I wanted to go downtown. I had been to Hong Kong once before and remembered an area full of lights where there were a bunch of great restaurants. I was delirious after the long twelve-hour flight and, momentarily forgetting where we were, I asked the driver, "Hey, bro, where's Chinatown?" He looked at me like I was crazy and snapped, "This is all Chinatown! You're in China." When I looked at Khalil, we couldn't help but laugh. One day there will have to be a comedy outtake version of *Return to Happiness*.

Once we were back on the plane and heading for our final destination, I could feel my dream beginning to take form. When we landed, the humidity in Bangkok was so intense after coming from winter in Vancouver that I immediately opened my suitcase once I was outside the airport so I could throw on some shorts and a shirt. The first thing anyone who travels to Thailand experiences upon arrival is the airport taxi men throwing bargain after bargain at you, hoping it's your first time there and you will bite on the first dib. I guess I stood out a bit since I was changing into shorts in the open while twenty-plus Thai cabbies screamed out, "RIDE WITH ME!" I knew I could get Khalil and I into town for about ten American dollars, so I refused the first few drivers.

Thailand has become a massive tourist destination in the past few years, so what once was a very cheap and poor country is now attracting people with more money; as a result, the prices everywhere but in the desolate regions have sky rocketed. While we were trying to find a cab at the right price, some creep approached Khalil and me to ask why we were filming. He thought I was a kook because I went off into my positivity speech. He just wanted to take a cab to wherever he could find the cheapest hookers. I told him to "Take a hike." He was obviously offended and barked at us, "You only live once!" God if he only knew I had lived many lifetimes, and I wasn't about to screw this one up!

Finally, a kind old gentleman accepted my offer to give us a ride. Off to the hotel we went. Khalil was filming everything and didn't miss a beat. We were in a foreign land with bright lights, massive billboards, and huge skyscrapers. I said right off the bat, "It's the JOURNEY. You almost just want to let it write itself!" We were both pumped. Khalil just kept saying, "This is insane, Ryan!" and this was only the beginning.

I felt right at home in Thailand (the land of smiles). The Thai people, despite the sex industry there and their poverty, are wonderful souls. Primarily Buddhists, the majority of the people will go out of their way to help you. I've been blessed in my time over there to make some lifelong friendships.

Khalil and I went to the hotel and jumped into the pool with enormous smiles on our faces as I tried to explain to him the magnitude of the massive city of Bangkok where the poorest of the poor lived amid plush hotels. Street vendors were everywhere. Of course, sin was represented—on Sukhumvit street in the Patpong district, ladies of the night go-go dance and sell their bodies to foreigners who come to Bangkok just for that reason. It made me sad to think of these girls who chose to sell their bodies. Prostitution and sex slavery had long been part of Thailand's dark side. Girls from small villages and even the big city would seduce drunk visitors with sex.

We weren't going to be in Bangkok for more than twenty-four hours since my mind was set on Khao Lak. I chose not to go out that night because I wanted to be fresh for the kids I would be meeting at the orphanage in two days, and it had been a long haul so far. But I insisted that Khalil go out and see firsthand how wild Bangkok can be at night. I was awoken early when he returned to the room, close to 5 a.m. He was in shock. He had been exposed to the dark side and had many girls solicit him for sex. He couldn't stop saying, "This is sooo wrong, Ryan!" I could only shake my head and agree that when you come to Southeast Asia, you need to be prepared for a total eye-opener! There was the good side and then the side I tried to ignore. I met many girls while in Thailand who were selling their bodies, and I always treated them with respect. They were people too; they were just lost, and in some ways, trying to find a way out. Numerous beggars were also along the roads, and my heart went out to them. Many were maimed and disfigured, perhaps on purpose, and put to work by the people who had hurt them. I saw an old blind man who had lost both his eyes, perhaps to acid; he tapped his cane on the ground while begging on his knees for money. These experiences were all new to Khalil, and they emotionally affected both of us, causing us to talk about how grateful we both were to have what we did.

We had a few hours the next morning before our 11 a.m. flight, so we grabbed a tuk-tuk, a type of taxi where the passengers are out in the open except for a roof. These pretty groovy vehicles cost less than an actual cab. We told our tuk-tuk driver to give us a tour of the city's core. I waved and smiled at everyone as Khalil filmed every smile and wave. We were having a blast and didn't get one nasty glare back from any of the locals. It was so hot that the soles of my brand new shoes stuck to the red paint on the floor of the tuk-tuk. The driver tried not to laugh when I told him we should get a deal since I figured it was fresh paint and hadn't dried. No dice, so I paid him two hundred baht (Thai currency, worth about five American dollars).

When we got back to the hotel, I met a big Russian man who came up and shook my hand. He was having a photo shoot for a new cologne he was launching. He said, "It drives women wild!" He asked to take my photo and he gave me a bottle. I think his cologne was actually a woman repellent because it smelled like bug spray, but he was a cool guy, so we gave him the old thumbs up and had a quick chat before taxiing off to the airport.

The airport was packed, but I hadn't felt this good in years. I couldn't stop smiling, and I guess when you have a guy following you around with a camera, you're going to get some onlookers. It was special, though, because kids were running up to me, jumping into my arms, and we were meeting families and monks as well. Bangkok airport is a major hub for many islands and other countries. We had the travel bug and this would be just the beginning of many airports and hotels during this adventure.

CHAPTER 7
KHAO LAK—EXPERIENCING LOVE

"Love can mend even the deepest unseen wounds. Love can heal. Love can console. Love can strengthen, and yes, love can make a change."
— Somaly Mam

God was on our side all right because we got seats with some leg room on the short flight to Phuket. We sat beside some guys from Italy who had laughed at me for doing a leg dance in celebration of our takeoff. Before we knew it...touchdown in Phuket! We quickly grabbed our bags and were once again bombarded with cab offers. I made an offer of fifty dollars and got a taker on the second bid. We made it to Khao Lak in just under two hours, and the drive was surreal. We saw several beach towns and a lot of palm trees. And, of course, many small villages that were devastated by the tsunami in 2004. Our driver spoke very limited English, but he was accommodating in helping us to find a hotel near the school where we would be visiting the next day.

Our hotel was across from the beach where the tsunami wave had hit. Now the beach was serene and beautiful. Our hotel wasn't the typical building but bungalow-style and in the heart of a lush jungle with beautiful gardens full of colorful flowers and a large pond where you could see fish swimming close to the clear water's surface. We met some other people in the hotel who were much older than us but also there for the same purpose—to help kids in need, to teach English, and to give back in any way they could. Khalil and I took some complimentary bikes owned by the hotel and explored the coastline. We then took some time to walk the beach. It was hard to imagine everything that had transpired when the big wave had struck some years earlier. The sunset was majestic, and the sky was tinted with a mixture of indigo, red, blue, and orange.

Chris had made a call to some amazing people with whom he'd developed close ties over the years, the owners of Dee Time, a travel and tour company. The owners had lost many family members in the tsunami, and they had known Chris' parents well since Khao Lak had been his parents' travel destination every Christmas. I called the travel company and spoke to a lady named Suk. She was happy to know we had arrived safely, and she was excited to make our visit special. The next morning, we took a cab to the travel center to meet Suk, her husband, and her brother. They treated us to an authentic Thai meal with some chilled coconut water.

Next, I had to learn what the kids in the orphanage needed the most. When I found out that seventy kids only had one soccer ball to share, it seemed only fitting that we load up with an abundance of balls and tennis rackets and as many cases of fresh drinking water as we could fit in the truck. On the travel center's wall, which had been made into a memorial, I saw pictures of Chris' parents and many others who had lost their lives in the tsunami. Guests who came to help kids and be a part of relief efforts were able to sign a guestbook to give thanks and appreciation, so I was able to give my gratitude to these lovely people who were making this a special day. It was tough to hold back the tears after hearing some of the horror stories, but after giving Suk a big hug and loading up with all our supplies for the kids, we knew good times were ahead because visiting the school was right around the corner.

The language barrier was a bit of a test upon arriving at the school. I found the kids instantly became magnetized to me as our old truck pulled up and we started to unload what we had brought for them. I was then introduced to the staff and principal, who were very kind and explained how hard it was for many of these kids who had never gotten to know their parents. We shared some laughs in the main office as I did my best to explain *Return to Happiness* to the principal. I told him that we stood for the universal truth of love and spreading happiness along our journey. When he told me he was fifty-seven, I ribbed him and told him age was only a number and that he looked much younger. All the staff shared in our laughs.

I was then led around the school and classrooms where I was able to give and receive some uplifting hugs from the kids and teachers. I was having the time of my life, and the day had barely even begun. These kids had so much love inside them despite what they had lost. I guess in my mind I figured they just didn't know any better. But I also saw the togetherness that they shared with each other. They all showed such good manners and respect because, as I found out later, visitors didn't come that often.

Now it was soccer time and these kids were pumped! I was equally excited, and the principal did such a good deed in letting these kids all out of class for an afternoon of fun. Before our big game, a group photo was only fitting. Chris had been right—I became a human jungle gym to these youngsters who proved to me in that moment that the best things in life are always free. Playing with these kids took me back to my own youth when I was almost always in the moment. Thoughts of Chris' parents, my own daughter, and all that had been lost years earlier echoed in my heart and soul.

After at least three hours of soccer, I was exhausted and drenched with sweat. The school was about to close for the day, so it was time for goodbyes—the hardest part. But I had learned that almost wherever you go with an open heart and mind, life rewards you with an incredible feeling beyond description. It wasn't what I gave to these kids; it was what they gave me. They gave me a love that will be ingrained in my soul forever. This meeting with them surely wouldn't be my last. I threw many of these kids high up in the air and caught them on the way down. In only a short time, our bond became one of the greatest gifts I had ever received in my life.

As we drove off in the truck, we pulled around the corner of the school where the kids were out of sight. I just shook my head, feeling like I was twelve years old again. Then I could hear a swarm of children screaming as they came running around the corner, yelling a loud "Gooooodbyyyeeeee!" They just kept on running after the truck as we pulled back onto the road toward the hotel.

I just couldn't stop laughing and talking about the kids who had made this day one I would cherish forever. When Suk's brother dropped us off, I thanked him for driving us and helping make it all possible. I knew he'd had just as much fun as we did, and he had even played goalie for a while.

The sun was so beautiful that after some food and a shower, Khalil and I walked down to the beach to film the serene water. Khalil had filmed some great shots at the school that day, capturing the love and how small deeds in life go such a long way. He had played some soccer as well, between takes. I just couldn't believe all the laughs, smiles, and thanks those precious young souls had given us. I knew that whenever in the future I might get a bit down, all I had to do was remember that day. As we walked along the beach, we reflected on all that had happened that day and thus far on our trip. Already, we were learning so much about ourselves and how unconditional love is the seed to a more harmonious planet.

That night, we rode our bikes down a winding road in almost pitch dark to a small village about five minutes away from our hotel. We were told the village was inhabited by "sea gypsies." In the village, we came upon a little store that sold fresh fruit. The owner was a man in his sixties. Right away, he saw the Thai tattoos I had on my chest and the Buddha on my shoulder. I had gotten them a few years back from my friend Koko, a local tattoo artist on the island of Ko Phi Phi. Both tattoos were done with bamboo in Thai writing. One said "Love" and the other "Good Life." The man invited us in for a meal on the house. His wife and daughter prepared a wonderful dinner for us, and he wouldn't take the money I offered him. He loaded us up with fresh mangosteen fruit and told us in broken English to "Have safe trip!" We met a bunch of the gypsies as well who all lived a simple life off the land and the fresh fish from the ocean. It was official—we were in paradise!

CHAPTER 8
PATONG—HEALTH

"The greatest wealth is health."
— Virgil

Now it was off to Patong to visit my good friend, the fierce Muay Thai fighter Kru Master Charm, whom I had met on a previous trip to Thailand. He was a very kind, gentle man outside the ring who took pride in helping others achieve optimal health and wellbeing. Charm was forty-two, but he looked not a day older than twenty-three.

Khalil and I were on rented mopeds, and of course, he had the camera in his backpack. We were ripping through the streets at high speed but I hadn't told Khalil where we were going. He was just following behind me since I knew the area very well. When I pulled into the Muay Thai gym, which was half outdoors, half indoors, Khalil was in shock! He thought I hadn't been there before, and he was intimidated by some of the fighters hammering away on heavy bags and skipping rope. But he felt a lot calmer when I was greeted with open arms by Charm and his friend

Jamon, a twenty-five time world champion fighter. Jamon was a proud but humble man just like Charm, whose dedication and work ethic showed not only in his physical body, but in the intense focus of his eyes.

Charm had taught me the basics of Thailand's national sport a few years earlier when I had visited Thailand, and he had gotten a real rise at being on film demonstrating some of his skills. The human body is very resilient and can be pushed to do amazing things when fueled by passion and desire. Charm was about fifty pounds lighter than my 200-pound frame, but he could turn me into a pretzel within the blink of an eye. Jamon was loving it as well, calling me "Big man!" His battle scars were proof that he had been in many intense ring wars in the past. Fighting was how he made his living and provided for his family. Khalil filmed some great training shots. We learned that they trained six hours a day with only a short rest around noon.

I've come to believe that whenever you focus with drive and determination, you will reach your true potential in whatever you strive for. It's very important to set goals and aim high in life because the more energy you put toward what you desire, the sooner the dream or goal will manifest. So it's my humble suggestion that if you have a dream or a goal, write it down and read it daily with emotionalized words. See and believe yourself already in possession of that which you desire. Words have great power, and once you feed your subconscious mind with emotional words, it will literally change your vibration and place you into action mode so you can achieve your goal. The more you think about your goals and make them an all burning obsession, the more momentum and speed will come in manifesting them. Evidence of your goals becoming reality will be all around you when you are truly open to receiving what you desire. The more you believe, the more you will attract the tools to make your dream crystallize into reality. Dreams are the beginning of reality, but they need to be backed by intense desire and belief.

The focused and positive attitude of these fighters was what stood out the most for me. It was a true blessing to witness how humble and gentle they were outside the ring. Eight fighters were training that day in what was not an ordinary gym. It was old and tattered, and the ring was worn out. The bags were beaten and aged as well. But each fighter had a respect for the others, and Charm told me that they would all go to one another's fights to cheer their fellow gym mates on. Upon my arrival, they showed respect to Khalil and me by stopping what they were doing to bow to us.

I was impressed by these fighters' determination to succeed in their skills and be healthy in mind and body. What are we without our health? A person can have all the money in the world, but without good health, how can anyone enjoy the richness and fullness of mind, body, and soul? I encourage everyone to incorporate habits of exercise and good eating habits into his or her life. Just like the good food that fuels our bodies, it's important to saturate our mental faculties with positive inspiration to get into a good feeling place. Your body is a temple, but it is also a perfect machine, manifested in god-form. Whatever god or power you believe in, that god wants all of us to succeed in life, and success all comes down to action! Exercise promotes blood flow and releases natural endorphins that are beneficial to achieving a happier state of being.

After my training session with these amazing men, Khalil and I took a ride down the coast where I intermingled with some great locals. I met this really cool little boy named Mook, who ran into my arms right away. His dad ran a little restaurant on the side of a cliff overlooking a small bay on the Adaman Sea. Khalil and I had to climb down a long set of steps to get to this restaurant, and when we did, we saw that the beach below was called "Paradise Beach." I was wearing blue swimming goggles for giggles and reactions, and Mook thought I was a real-life clown. I love nothing more than making kids laugh and smile; their innocence and pureness hits hard and turns me into butter.

Khalil was steadfast on getting a "go-pro" camera—a high definition and waterproof camera you can take anywhere—to film much of our adventure. Then I could strap one onto my helmet and capture exactly what I was seeing while riding on the moped. Khalil and I had a heck of a time finding one in Phuket, but we did finally track one down at a dive and surf shop run by a cool Aussie man in his mid-fifties who had moved to Thailand close to twenty years earlier. He said his main source of income these days came from selling these cool little cameras.

We hadn't been in Thailand long, but I had overlooked that my base tan from hitting the indoor tanning beds wasn't exactly a great one. I learned it the hard way, of course—I got absolutely scorched that day after being on the moped for close to five hours as we traveled to Patong. Oh yeah, Asian sunburn was no fun! Just the touch of Khalil's finger on my back, which took the brunt of my burn, was an agony. I had to lie face down on the bed as a wee bit of sunstroke set in. Khalil ran to the drugstore to get some aloe vera lotion, which felt somewhat cooling as he rubbed it in.

When Khalil thought it would be amusing to capture my burn on film, I just looked at the camera with my bloodshot eyes and said, "Take me to the burn ward; I'm crisped; look at my back." We both couldn't help but laugh. He made a short video we never released called "Asian sunburn," on which I stated, "Asian sunburns are no fun; make sure you be careful of the intense sun, and if you have sunblock, well, wear some!" I struggled to catch a few hours of sleep since my head looked like a tomato as well.

But we were here to film, so nothing was going to hold us back from exploring the night life of Patong, which attracts people from all over with its bright lights, amazing beaches, and around the clock entertainment. I strapped the go-pro on my helmet and scooted my moped around the city in attempts to capture some cool shots. Khalil followed behind me in a tuk-tuk. We had perfect timing because we came along a fire display that occurs nightly on Patong Beach. After our tour, I came home to dump off the moped, and then we walked through the main area of town, Bangla Road. My god, the things you see on this street really do a number on the mind. From go-go dancers and lady boys to thousands of tourists from all walks of life, everyone is getting into the party.

We didn't spend that much time other than a quick walk down the street. I then saw that people were setting flaming flying lanterns into the sky; it's a tradition in Thailand to dedicate these lanterns to loved ones, past and present. So I fired one up myself and said some good prayers for all the people who had lost their lives in the 2004 tsunami and especially for Chris' parents.

By then, a lightning storm was coming in over the distant mountains and a thunderstorm was in store for the city in less than an hour. Before the storm hit, I came across a peace rally. I chatted with a few police officers who told me it was a regular event the locals hold in an attempt to spread goodness into the community. A kind man asked me to say a few words into the loud speaker, so I did my best to send out some good vibes. "Hello everyone in Patong Beach! I just want to say that I love you very much, and I wish you all love, health, and happiness. I LOVE YOU!" The crowd of about 300 cheered and applauded me. I'm not too sure they all fully understood my words, but they could tell by my smile that my intentions were heartfelt! I got some high-fives and more hugs and smiles as I made my way through the crowd.

The next morning, we were up very early as we wanted to see the town in a quieter state. It was just after 6 a.m. and

Patong was like a ghost town. We saw people who had been partying all night, stumbling to who knows where.... The job of cleaning up Bangla Street was a tough one. Garbage trucks went along with workers throwing big black garbage bags full of empty beer bottles into the back of the truck. I then came upon a small group of people who had candles lit, and one of the Thai gentleman asked to read my palm. I thought, "Hey, why not? Maybe it will be good for the film." When the man started telling me of my past, he wasn't far off from the truth. He said I had been through many struggles in life, but now through a new way of looking at life, I was finding peace. He also said my sixth sense was very active now and that I would see life manifesting in exact accordance with how I focused my thoughts. He spoke perfect English. I took what he had to say with a grain of salt and handed him a couple of hundred baht for his "wisdom" before leaving him. He concluded by telling me that I would live a very long life. Then he looked at me very intensely and said I had much work left to do in this world before I leave. Who knows? Maybe he was just playing it up in front of the camera. But whatever the case, in my evolving awakening process, I have always tried to be in the present moment. I mean, if you think and feel it, the here and now is all we ever have. There's no time for worry and fears because the more we fear and worry, the more life will hold us back from experiencing the beauty and power our universe possesses. All we really have is today, so why not make it a good one and spread as much happiness to others as we can? And when my eyes open tomorrow, if I receive that blessing, I will give the world my best as I see fit. Every day, every second is a gift.

The following morning would be our last in Patong. We were off to the majestic island of Ko Phi Phi, which is part of the Phi Phi Islands and commonly referred to simply as Phi Phi. Just before 6 a.m., I was on my way to the hotel lobby to check out when I crossed paths with an old monk who must have been in his eighties. I could see the wisdom in his eyes, and our eyes locked as we gravitated toward each other. Good thing Khalil was right behind me to catch it all on film—things were just flowing. This old monk grabbed my right wrist and put a handcrafted bracelet on me. He started laughing and saying, "HAPPY, HAPPY, OHHH, HAPPY!" It didn't surprise me because my mind was focused on being happy, and I could sense that he picked up on my thought vibrations. We are constantly attracting to ourselves what we are thinking about, and this response made my day! That bracelet hasn't left my wrist since. The pieces of the puzzle were now starting to fall into place; this film wouldn't be a documentary about the making of a travel show—now we were creating a story about being happy.

CHAPTER 9
PHI PHI—THE SIMPLICITY OF LIFE

"Life is not complex. Life is simple, and the simple thing is the right thing."
— Oscar Wilde

After we checked out early, the hotel staff had a cab waiting for us and the driver lined up ferry tickets from Chalong Bay's ferry and fishing port. It was an hour drive to the port, and our ferry departed at 9 a.m. Our time spent in Patong had been awesome—we'd learned a lot about health, mind, and body. And the locals had embraced us with much affection. Now the journey was to a small island.

When we arrived at the port, we saw that it was jam-packed with tourists taking off to many different islands off Phuket. Khalil and I were blessed enough to get onto the boat early to ensure good seats. But we chose to spend the majority of the two-hour boat ride on top of the boat's starboard where we could capture all the scenic views en route to our destination.

Our departure at nine was late when compared to the

multitudes of old fishing vessels already coming and going on the bay with early catches of abundant seafood, which supplied many of Phuket's tourist areas. The seafood in Thailand is amazing, and in most cases, it's always caught that day. The old boats also housed many of the fishermen. As I waved at many of the workers coming and going from the port, the friendly fishermen smiled and waved back.

The short doorways on the ferry got the best of me as I smashed my head hard and nearly knocked myself out—a great way to start the day, knocking a little sense into my brain while earning a wild goose egg as my forehead started to swell. A few people saw and heard the loud thump of my head ringing off the doorway. I tried my best to laugh it off. Khalil, of course, put the camera on me as one Thai lady rubbed my forehead, checking out the lump. I made a joke to her, saying, "They need to raise the doorways on this boat. I need to talk to the guy who runs the show around here." She just smiled since I'm sure she didn't understand a word I said.

Up on the front deck, about five minutes into our trip, we met many different people who were taking pictures. I met a really nice couple from the United States who was spending one year exploring the world. They were on their last two months of the excursion and said that Southeast Asia had been their favorite place so far. We met a really nice family from Hong Kong who insisted we take a group photo. The vibe on the boat was great. What I find so cool about traveling is that people often become very open, and you meet people from so many different countries and cultures. I always do my best to get to know people from all walks of life. It intrigued me to know what drove them to travel and go on their own personal journeys. Even though we all come from different places in the world, we all share a oneness, a connectedness, no matter how far away we live from one another. Because of air travel, human beings are discovering how small the world really is.

The Phi Phi Islands also had been devastated by the tsunami, taking an estimated 4,000 lives of locals and tourists. Ko Phi Phi itself is a small but very special island; it boasts no cars, and the only means of transportation is riding a bicycle. People explore the magnificent surrounding bays with its baby blue, crystal clear water. Diving is a big attraction as well.

I had visited the island with my father a few years previously, but since then, the island had become increasingly more popular with travelers because of its immense beauty. Accommodations on the island were fairly inexpensive, but we found a room in one of the nicer bungalows on the side of one of two cliffs on each side of the island. A room with two beds at high season cost us forty-five dollars. On my previous visit, it had been a lot cheaper, but now Thailand's tourist industry was booming like never before. The country is saturated with countless tourists, some of whom don't always respect the land and its gentle people. However, the Thai people have taken advantage of this situation, preying on many intoxicated tourists who are there for the big party. I've been blessed to experience both sides of the spectrum. The party is always going full steam in Thailand. The islands of Ko Phi Phi and Koa Pha Ngan sell buckets of potent Thai whiskey! Their whiskey is more of a narcotic than a beverage, and it can drive madness into many people who find themselves in trouble after ingesting too much. It wouldn't be an exaggeration to say, "I've seen it all" there on the beaches, which play host to big parties with loud music and bright lights—parties that go nonstop until the sun comes up.

But I was here for a different purpose this time. My once wild ways were a thing of the past, although I laughed wholeheartedly at myself for escaping the wrath of my past mischief. My new intoxicants of choice were laughter, exercise, and trying to be as creative as possible through channeling good energy every step of the way. I wanted to capture on film the simplicity of life that the locals have on this island.

The elderly man who ran the hotel was new to my eyes. At first glance, he looked like he would judge me by my exterior until he saw my Thai tattoos. Then he warmed right up to me as Elvis music played in the background. He grabbed my hand and proceeded to do a dance while laughing loudly. He pretended he was pulling a rope to the sound of Elvis' classic "I'm All Shook Up." Khalil filmed away. The man paid no attention to the camera as we double high-fived, and he explained that all the happiness he experiences he channels from his brain's sixth sense, a field of consciousness we can channel through unknown sources beyond the five senses that makes us aware of reality on a greater level. Since my sixth sense had been active for me from an early age, I understood exactly what this elderly man was referring to. I had read years earlier in Napoleon Hill's book *Think and Grow Rich* that the sixth sense was the "door to the temple of wisdom." I believed this statement to be true as my "higher self" had, in most cases, always warned me of danger lurking in the future. It was that source of energy that always led me into making the right choices, especially in states of emergency when my brain had to be stimulated and highly receptive to make sound choices beyond the reasoning faculty of normal consciousness. In many cases, as I look back, if I hadn't depended on my "sixth sense," I suspect I wouldn't be alive.

The staff at the hotel, including all the cleaning ladies, was so pleasant. I had never been so "in tune," and I was learning what it meant to be a deliberate creator of my experience with little effort. The more I was relaxed and just went with the flow of life, the more happiness I allowed into my consciousness and my field of awareness. On the way to the room up a steep grade of stairs, one of the cleaning ladies approached me and gave me a big hug. Her open friendliness and affection caused me to reflect how different my life was now from when I had been living in the darkness. I had always said what I thought, and if I didn't get my way, I'd be angry and resentful. I had always been trying to prove I was "better" than other people. Now, the only thing coming out of my mouth was a reminder to me, "It's a lot easier to be nice and gentle than angry and mental." These weren't just words; they came from an inner source of love that I wished to pass on to everyone with whom I came into contact. In my past, I had seen too many unfortunate episodes of violence. Life is meant to be lived fully and we are meant to experience beauty no matter where we are in the world. The only thing that ever holds us back from a state of wellbeing and happiness is our resistant thoughts. For many years now, I have written daily with love everything for which I was truly grateful, and one of them is always "love for all of humanity."

Once Khalil and I were settled into our room, I took a walk to a scenic point where you can see as far as your eyes will let you. The sunsets on the point were surreal. On the way back, I asked a few people what made them happy. One gentleman, who had a hut on the mountainside, said, "You know here is very happy! No cars...no beep, beep. If I get bored, I go fishing, take swim. Don't worry; be happy; no problem." He grabbed my left hand and proceeded to guide me into a little dance, making up his own words to Bob Marley's "Don't Worry, Be Happy!" As I left him, I expressed my thanks and said with a big grin, "Thanks for the show!" He had made me laugh, but he was just a simple man who had everything he needed within a short walk.

I was here on the island of Phi Phi to capture for others the simplicity of life and the appreciation of family that these people had. During this visit, I spent a lot of time reflecting on my family and the pain I had put them through. My mom had always loved me unconditionally.

When I had been mixed up with the wrong people, she had spent years of sleepless nights wondering where I was, or whether I was even alive. My life had been a tornado, and I never knew where I would end up after the party began. If I were in my home city, the party never ended early, and I'd often not get home from an after-hours club until noon the next day. My mom would have a special Sunday dinner I was committed to, but 90 percent of the time, I would miss it, with my phone turned off or the battery dead or lost. The few times when I did show up, I was beat down hard and always needed a few drinks to take off the edge. My mom would be in tears and just shake her head in fear. My dad would become angry for how I was making my mom feel. And I was just plain embarrassed by how I was letting my behavior run my life. Now I thanked God that I did not have to live like that. Now I was extreme in other ways, being a healthy role model who gave hope to others who were in deep despair. I wore my emotions close to the surface and I was not one bit ashamed because it was the true nature of my being. It's okay to cry; that's why our creator gave us tears in the first place.

After a walk through the small town, I felt the need to express my gratitude for my life on this planet in front of the camera. I couldn't express my emotions in any other way than utter sincerity. I said, "Every day, every moment that my heart beats...I don't take any day for granted—none of them! Life is so special!" This transformation of self that is always expanding and ever changing is a gift. From my perspective, I felt the need to tell my story! To give hope to anyone in a state of fear and sadness. I wanted to show people how life's blessings are always on the other side of our fears and disbelief.

That first day in Phi Phi was windy, but I wanted to get out into a boat and explore the surrounding bays, especially Maya Bay and the Viking Caves, where people had been living for many years, but tourists were forbidden to enter.

Monkey Island was a short ride from the shore where families of monkeys would take advantage of tourists, persuading people to feed them all kinds of different fruit. When a light tropical storm came up, the sea became very choppy, so our boat ride was cut short. I still paid the skipper generously. As the storm began, I soaked up the warm rain on my face. The forces of nature are something I respect with all my being because we are always at Mother Nature's mercy, and some things, like our boat ride, just weren't meant to be.

I was greatly anticipating my reunion with my old pal Koko, the local tattoo artist, so as soon as the short storm subsided, I went and surprised him with a warm embrace. He was a kind soul who knew everyone on this small island. I wanted to get my last tattoo and capture the process on film to express my love and gratitude for my family. They had given me the gift of life and always been there for me no matter what, doing their best to take away my fears and anxieties that still worked against me from my past. I was trying as much as possible to let go of everything I had put myself through in my past, but having seen such a grim side of life, it was often hard to control where my mind went. It would be fair to say I was experiencing some post-traumatic stress. But everything I was doing now to help others, coupled with my family's love and support, was moving me beyond those memories. I knew the tables of thought could be turned for me if I took action to do so. That's where the true power always lies—in ACTION! And the more momentum we gain in the direction of expecting the good, the more people start to believe in it and in us. Best of all, we live in an age where new enlightenment is being shed onto universal energy. People want to be happy and they are changing the world to make it so!

Koko hooked up an old Thai boat, nicknamed "a one-tailer," for us to use the next day. It was "Thai yachting" at its best. He also introduced us to his pal Bao, who lived in a small handmade hut behind the bamboo tattoo parlor. Bao was shy and gentle. Everything he had in his life was within an arm's reach. He did what he loved. We arranged to meet Boa at nine o'clock the next morning for our boat ride.

In the morning, we arrived a few minutes early to try to find Boa. He immediately popped out of the hut, just awoken from his night sleep, and he greeted me with a massive smile, showing his crooked teeth. I asked him, "Are you all gassed up, all ready to go?" He nodded that he was.

Today, the water was calm. Boa let me drive the very long tail boat out into the sea. Three of us were out there in the open sea experiencing a great moment. When we stopped the boat, I said a few words in my head to my family. My dad, who had battled his way back from heart surgery, was such a motivating factor for me to push on in life! He'd taught me always to be the best I could be and never to sweat the small stuff. I have to confess that if it hadn't been for my parents, I wouldn't be writing these lines.

We spent a long day in the boat, exploring the bays. I kept yelling at the top of my lungs to everyone in sight, "Are you seeing how beautiful this is? Look around you!" The swimmers and people in other boats nodded in agreement. I yelled loud, "Woooooooooooo!" and Khalil and Boa matched my screams with even louder ones. What a blessing! I got another sunburn to add to my collection, but the sunset made up for it. We pulled onto the beach at dark with a full moon shining over our heads. I bought Boa some cold beer and gave him twenty dollars and he was happier than heck.

I needed a quick nap, and then it would be time to see Koko for my new ink. My parents had taught me at a young age that if I never stopped believing in myself, I would always be great at anything to which I put my mind. Isn't it odd how so many of us get to a certain point where we think life should be difficult? The truth is that everything along our journey is a test. There's nothing in the world that will ever hit us as hard as life itself because it's always a mystery. When we are younger, we are a lot different and life is usually easier. Then we get to where we have to go out into the world, and it's like one giant proving ground of what we can or can't be, what we can achieve or accumulate. But at the end of the day, the one universal power that governs all things wants us to succeed. And because we have so many talents and gifts to give back to the world, wouldn't it just make sense to be less hard on ourselves, to look at the sunny side of everything, and give our shining light back to the world? Feel how good it feels when everyone is happy and smiling around you. Laughing until tears come out of my eyes is the best feeling. Whoever God may be, I believe God put us on this earth to experience emotions on all levels, including suffering. How else would we know what it feels like to be alive if we didn't feel emotion? Emotions are the driving force behind everything in this world. They are what feed our creative endeavors, lead us to love, and to *be* love. And to experience pain as well. If we didn't experience pain, we wouldn't understand what joy feels like.

I was one of the blessed kids who had grown up with love around me all the time. I was taught by my parents to share everything that was good and always to be honest. Now after many years of being their son, I realized on such a deep level all the sacrifices my parents had made in order for me to grow up being happy. I had played every sport in our community, and one or both of my parents would always drive me to practice or a game after work. Many times, I would have hockey practice at 5 a.m. But there Mom or Dad would be—a quick bowl of cereal and it was straight to the rink. Then they would have to work all day to pay for the sports I played, the clothes I wore, and the food my brother and I ate. They did the very best they could. If they couldn't get me to a game, they'd arrange for me to carpool with another kid's mom, dad, or family. My parents were ultra-organized, and that's what made our family work in harmony.

Think of all the circumstances and situations that had to occur just so you could have your being on this planet? The numbers, facts, and figures are too mind-boggling; it's impossible to realize how many pieces to the puzzle had to be put together just so you could be here. What a blessing life is! My mom taught me to live every day like it's my last because that's how she lived. She learned to appreciate life after being in a car crash when she was sixteen. Her face was so badly scarred that she was in the hospital for close to a year. My late grandfather didn't miss a day seeing mom in the hospital during that duration, showing her his unconditional love and unwavering faith to help her move past the tragedy. All these things in life do happen; "big" or "small," we put the size and scope on the event's magnitude. Every second of our lives is a "life experience," and it's the people who make up our outer world that make us feel good inside. If my mom hadn't survived and my grandpa hadn't been there for her, my parents would have never met and I wouldn't have been born.

My parents met on a blind date and were engaged six months later. Dad wasn't about to let this woman slip away. I'm happy about that one! So is my brother, my daughter, and thousands of others who have crossed my parents' paths over the years. The evolution of our species is continuous expansion. I barely lived when I was born because the umbilical cord was wrapped so tightly around my neck that my head was blue. But I made it, and on that day when I came into the world, I had a path stretched before me like I never could have dreamed.

As I write this, tears are welling up in my eyes.... I could go on for pages about how my parents have helped to make my life worth living. And to all those parents who sacrifice and give unconditional love to their kids, parents who adopt, or people who mentor a youth, I salute you! You can never know how much your actions mean to the world.

My point here is that every one of us, even every insect and animal, is here to serve a purpose. Without the guidance of great people around me, I wouldn't have discovered a purpose for myself. And in many instances, we will serve many purposes in our time on earth.

Koko had told me to come about nine that evening for my tattoo—I say "about" because island time is different than back home. There are not a whole lot of clocks on the island. Every day was really laid back, and Koko, who hadn't left the island in eight years, didn't want to clutter his mind with the busyness of a big city like Bangkok. He told me that as a devout Buddhist, he just liked to keep it simple. I learned a lot about the simplicity of life by watching how the local islanders lived. Koko and I had developed an instant bond when we first met; he had a jovial way about him; he had long hair and was skinny, but his smile lit up the room.

When I arrived "about" 9 p.m., he was ready for me. He got out the Thai dictionary so I could design my tattoo. I found the letters I would be using: G for my dad, Grant; C for my mom, Cindy; another G for my brother, Greg; and, of course, S for my angel, Sadie. And my heart told me to put the sign for infinity or the infinite around the initials to bind the love I had for my family on my upper back forever. My design was unique because I used all Thai characters for the writing. I'm not going to sugarcoat the process either—bamboo tattoos are twice as painful as the norm. But I took the pain with a smile, and to distract me from the pain, a little boy from the neighborhood fed me parts of a dessert crepe with chopsticks because he could tell I fancied it.

When Koko had finished with giving me my new tattoo, Khalil and I walked down to the far end of the island where the locals were entertaining hundreds of onlookers with an epic fire show. The vibe was electric as families and their kids danced to the art of fire dancing and loud music. I talked to a few of the performers, who told me that during high season, this was a nightly event unless there was a thunderstorm. They made their money on tips. Everywhere I looked in the crowd, people were smiling in amazement. The vibe was palpable, and it was one of those moments when I wished time would just stand still.

The next morning, we were up early to get the first ferry. The small town was dead at 6 a.m. except for a few breakfast spots and, of course, the small hotel and bungalow lobbies. After we checked out, one of the workers insisted on helping us carry our gear to the busy pier where people would be coming and going. But I told him to relax; we were big strong boys accustomed to lugging around our bags. We had packed pretty lightly, considering how long we intended to be in Thailand.

We had planned to go to Bali next, but after some locals on the beach the previous day had told us about Laos and that we couldn't miss it, the decision to go there next became fixed in our hearts. We would take the ferry back to Phuket, stay one more night in Patong, and then get the earliest flight out the following morning to a small town in Laos called Luang Prabang. It would be my first time there, so I was excited. I had heard it was much more inexpensive and underdeveloped. People we spoke to compared it to what Thailand was like twenty years earlier.

The ferry ride back was quiet since a lot of the people aboard hadn't caught much sleep the night before. Khalil and I took the front bow of the boat because, as usual, we didn't want to miss anything. The light wind on my face felt amazing. I was a long way from home, but I had never felt so at one with myself and my purpose. I was seeing happiness everywhere, and it mostly came from living a simple life. I was pondering many thoughts at this point, and while we had a basic plan for the trip, I realized we could also be spontaneous, letting the plan change quickly, depending on what kind of sound travel advice we got from other travelers.

I also was so happy that on this trip, my travel companion wanted this beautiful experience to be created into a unique piece of cinematic art. You really get to know a person when you travel with him. Khalil and I closely bonded, and like the couple of emotional saps we were, we talked in depth about how much we just wanted to inspire others—he, through his music and creative mind, and me, well, I had my own style—I always just started with my smile and tried to give good energy through my actions and audible words on camera. We seldom did any second takes. We were gorilla shooting this whole production on the fly. It was go, go, go...and if we were to fake anything, it just wouldn't work. We knew from the get-go that if we were going to be happy with the final outcome, it had to be fueled with persistence and action. The action had to be nonstop to get the audience's attention. It had to be raw and authentic!

CHAPTER 10
LUANG PRABANG—THE UNIVERSAL MIND

"All that we are is the result of what we have thought. The mind is everything. What we think, we become."
— Buddha

It was a short flight to Luang Prabang. A really small plane carried us over countless rice fields and an abundance of cool mountains. I always loved the window seat. When we arrived, getting through security was a breeze; the airport was very small, and of course, tuk-tuks and taxi drivers waited patiently for customers. It was different here, though. They weren't in your face trying to drive hard bargains. Here we went to them. I locked eyes with a character of a driver with whom I shared a hilarious moment. I told him to get into the driver's seat and tried pushing him into it. He knew I was joking and played it right up. We both were being like kids. And he then crammed me into the back, saying, "Customer first; you the boss!"

The people who had told us about Laos were bang on. It was a tranquil place with temples a plenty, most dating far back in history, and peaceful monks getting along with their day. When I say monks, I don't mean a few here and a few there! This town was like a monk convention. Many monks had chosen to live here and practice the path to enlightenment.

We had a tough time finding living quarters and were a little let down not to have found a place along the mighty Mekong River, but just up the way, we found a perfect place. It was a small family-owned guesthouse and the people running it were so hospitable. Khalil and I looked at each other in amazement when we were told it only cost ten American dollars per night. That meant we would each get our own room for the first time in a few weeks. There was no bad blood between us, but everyone needs his space. Khalil, also being an artist, needed some time alone to design flyers for Electro Swing music, a music scene in which he was actively involved, including throwing festivals and parties. Being a DJ and cameraman are just two of Khalil's multiple talents.

That first night, we went and saw another amazing red and orange sun fall behind the mountains. I guess I'd reached that stage in my life where I could sit still enough and really take in the powerful force of the sun, with all it gives us to live and the colors it lets us see.

The night market was a big deal in L.B. You can find so many great clothes there for men and women for next to nothing. Shirts and comfortable pants were no more than two dollars. That's why we hadn't packed heavily for the trip—we knew everything we would need would be found overseas. They have these massive buffets where people eat on picnic tables. Two dollars for all your stomach desires. And as a bonus, all the food is organic. BBQ chicken breasts, fish, noodles, every fresh vegetable known to man. Khalil and I just looked at each other and shook our heads.

I wanted to film all this so everyone could feel this sense of pureness. The people there work hard to make everything an enchanting experience. And for the beer drinker, well, a big local beer goes for a buck. So if you're reading these lines, you better get to Laos before it changes like Thailand has because it's only a matter of time.

After dinner, we stopped off at a coffee shop and people-watched for a while. We met two really sweet girls from Quebec, Alexandra and Marie, who sat beside us. I said, "*Bonjour*" [hello], but Khalil picked it up from there since he lived in Montreal and French was his native tongue. The girls' English was a bit broken, but Khalil and the girls did their best to include me, and I did my best with my grade three level of French. We exchanged travel stories, and the girls loved the idea of our happiness adventure. They had been best friends since they were little girls, and they had been traveling for many months. They ordered these massive pancakes that I had to help them eat; I didn't need much convincing since the pancakes were topped with blueberries and whipped cream. After about an hour of laughing, we all decided to go to the bowling alley on the outskirts of town. We went down a dusty dark road in the back of a tuk-tuk. It was bumpy so, of course, I banged my head hard on the vehicle's low roof. The girls and Khalil laughed while I added another goose egg to my collection.

The bowling alley was old, and I'm not sure whether it was always a bowling alley, but it served its purpose. Only one other group was bowling there, and our tuk-tuk driver said he would just take a nap while we had our fun. And fun we had—the girls got the hang of it after a few gutter balls and some amateur pointers from Khalil and me. The alley was a bit slanted, but hey, we were in a small town in Southeast Asia doing something I doubt most people do when they come to Laos. We teamed up, a boy and girl per team, and Khalil and Marie took the prize. He relished his victory. I could see now that Khalil had a competitive side to him, and I liked it! It told me a lot about his character. Most successful people are born with that desire to win, not lose.

I didn't sleep well that night because when we got back to the guesthouse, more people had arrived from other parts of the country and Southeast Asia. We stayed up and got acquainted with our new friends. Then at 2 a.m., I remembered how, every morning, starting about 6 a.m., hundreds of monks walk the streets of Luang Prabang to receive offerings from locals and tourists. This tradition dates back to when Buddhism was first introduced to Laos. So I hopped into my room for a few hours of shut-eye. Marie and Alexandra planned on coming that next morning but ended up sleeping in. I had no choice about getting up, though, because not only was I intrigued and fascinated, but I needed to capture the monks on film. I banged on Khalil's room and got him up. He took delight in filming me in the morning. All I could say to the camera was "There's a reason why my eyes look like two coals in a snow bank." It was monk morning in Luang Prabang. So in the pitch dark, with sunlight at least an hour and half away, we tracked up to the main street. A lot of people were patiently awaiting the monks' arrival. The monks ranged in age from just four-years-old to the very elderly. We were told to offer them rice and fruit, and that the offering would be their only meal for the day. The rest of their day was spent in chanting and meditation.

I admired the monks for their devotion to meditation because I had been studying its benefits myself. Meditation has the ability to connect one with the universal mind. It benefits overall wellbeing and has been proven to strengthen the immune system. I know through studying the working principles of the mind that whenever I get emotionally involved with any desire and ask the universe for that which I truly want, I can feel the vibration of my physical body changing. The only requests that are answered by infinite intelligence or source energy are those where we send thought-energy with emotion and faith to the subconscious mind. That thought-energy causes the physical body to vibrate at a certain frequency; that frequency then attracts, through the medium of the ether, the physical equivalent of what we ask. The ether is the void between all the planets and stars suspended in our view, and this space is very much alive. It carries the wireless waves through radio, TV, and telephones all across the world. We often hear "Be careful what you ask for because you always get it!" Well, I believe that to be a very true statement. The answer isn't that complicated because most of us humans are so preoccupied with thinking about the lack of what we want instead of believing we will receive with positive certainty what we ask for. The majority of times we need to keep plugging our desires into our subconscious repeatedly with affirmations; then, it's only a matter of time before we see the manifestation of the object or person we desired and requested through the vibrations of our thought-energy. Such meditation takes discipline and persistence. Years ago, one of my friends suggested that I should meditate. I had tried, but I could never stay still and focused. Now I concentrate and make it a daily practice because it benefits anyone who puts the effort forward to connect to his source and visualize that which he wants in life. My mind used to be so busy, but now with the practice of meditation, I have been able to silence my mind so that very little bothers me. I highly recommend anyone who has a dream he or she wants to manifest to get into the practice of meditation and visualization for at least fifteen minutes a day.

Meditation helps us to keep our emotions not only under control but to use them for our benefit. We are entirely run on our emotions, which are manifestations of the energy we are vibrating. People pick up on energy!

Especially sensitive people. And the generation we live in now is shedding even more enlightenment on how we are run by unseen powers and forces that we can draw into our existence. There's nothing in the world that we can't possess; every resource has been gifted to us by our creator. The power we all possess inspires me with awe because we can create from the formless in a very short time. But for me now, it's all about beautiful relationships with like-minded people. I literally can focus on a subject for a few minutes and immediately see like thoughts and ideas surrounding that subject, injecting themselves into the creative faculty of my imagination. It took me some time to get a good grip on this process. But think of the human mind as being like a radio broadcasting signal. We send out thoughts and like thoughts come back. To go a step farther, consider when you're with a group of like-minded people who are all on the same vibration. The group is almost supercharged with thought-energy so everyone in the group feeds off everyone else. That's why surrounding yourself with positive like-minded people is so important to development in anything. When we can all come into alignment harmoniously, we can create what seem to be miracles. And the best part is that it is fun. There's no magic here. This knowledge came from personal observations by great teachers like Napoleon Hill, and I have acted on those observations so that I've been blessed to experience this process myself; I've found the power of manifestation to be amazingly true, and I practice it daily.

The monks were a bit late this particular morning, so I joked with a man from China, asking him, "Is there a big bell that wakes all the monks up?" He took me seriously, so I shouldn't have been so sarcastic; the next thing I knew, he was checking with his wife and said he would let me know. I told him that if the monks were late, I was going to go wake them up myself, and I asked whether he wanted to come with me. He pondered the idea for a second, but then in the distance, the monks came into sight. Hundreds of monks in single file walked through the town. I'm sure they were very grateful for the offerings, but they did not look overly happy—in essence, they had become a tourist attraction. And I heard later that many of the monks from this region have moved to more desolate places where they are left alone.

Later on that particularly hot day, I would end up being invited to a monastery. And I found out quickly that monks can have a great sense of humor. Filming everything was part of the norm now for us, and since we weren't forcing anyone to do anything, it was all in good fun. I think one monk in particular liked being on camera and wanted to put on a show for Khalil. He caught me off-guard when he started spraying me down with a hose. He laughed as he soaked me down, and on such a hot day, I actually found it refreshing. These monks didn't mind having fun in front of the camera, and we all laughed about it. I think it made that young monk's day.

When we got back to our guesthouse, I got my daily exercise by skipping rope for half an hour. Khalil laughed as I next proceeded to do my many sets of push-ups, a daily ritual on this trip since gyms were hard to find in the little towns. The girls and Khalil and I had heard about an amazing chain of waterfalls an hour outside of town, so when they came over, we decided to make the trip. It would give us a chance to strap on the go-pro and capture the countryside, filled with farm after farm of livestock, chickens, and, of course, rice! We had a really fun drive to the waterfall, filming the whole ride as we laughed away. When we stopped at a welcoming farmer's home so I could pee, he asked whether I wanted to ride on top of one of his many buffalo. Heck, I was always up for whatever came my way, so on top of the buffalo I went. I nicknamed her Darlene and joked that she was my new girlfriend. The farmer laughed—we all did at the poor buffalo's expense. I was probably going to be eating part of her or her brother over the course of the next few days at one of the all-you-can-eat buffets.

We got to the trailhead, which led to the many pools and waterfalls. It was such a contrast from the main city. The waterfalls were just perfect, and standing underneath them was like being in a birdbath. The water was just the perfect temperature. There were rope swings so people could swing high into the air, scream at the top of their lungs, and plunge into the water. Cameras were flashing to capture so many people enjoying this sanctuary. We were warned that some wild bears were also in the area, so if approached by one, we should just stay put and not run.

I wanted to go to the source of the main waterfall at the top of the big mountain. Stairs had been built to make it easier for people to get to the top. During the climb, one of my sandals broke and I tripped, taking all the skin off my right anklebone, but I kept trudging along. When we reached the top, it was as if we had conquered Everest. The view was exhilarating. I tried my best to sum up the feelings I had inside of me on camera, but I kept laughing because of the spill I had taken forty-five minutes earlier.

We had done some research on riding elephants because we had heard that in many parts of Southeast Asia they were mistreated and used only as tools to make money. When we mentioned elephants to the girls, they told us about an elephant sanctuary in Laos where the elephants were treated very well, bathed, and fed, while being allowed to live like they were in their natural wild habitat. So the next day, we took a riverboat to the elephant sanctuary. The elephants looked healthy there and had much more color to them than some of the ones we had refused to ride in Thailand. It made me upset to see people in Thailand use these gentle beasts as simply money tools and take the liberty of smashing hooks into their heads so they could control them. But now, we were in elephant paradise. We were able to swim with these gentle beasts, and they actually dunked us right into the river's depths, which was refreshing considering the heat, and most of all, it was fun. We then trekked through jungle trails where we saw tropical birds and monkeys in abundance.

We stayed in Laos for ten days. We didn't want to leave because we had formed really close friendships with the people who ran the guesthouse. They loved that I made an effort to cook meals for them, whether it be dinner or lunch. Our breakfast, which consisted mostly of barbecued chicken on a stick of all things, we usually ate down by the Mekong River. Our next destination on the map was supposed to be Bali, Indonesia because I had a friend in Ubud there who was a DJ. She had told me how beautiful it was there, and I had seen pictures and heard enchanting tales of its uniqueness. But the day before we planned to purchase our tickets, I checked my Facebook page and saw that an old friend of mine had been doing charity advocacy work in Cambodia. Serinda Swan and I had known each other for about ten years, but I hadn't talked to her in at least four. I had seen her life take on a new shape as she launched a film career. We had met in a clothing store where I used to shop, and I knew right away that she was a kind soul. She always had a smile on her face that went hand-in-hand with her bubbly personality. Serinda had a head on her shoulders—she knew what she wanted in life. What most impressed me about her, however, was her compassion for and kindness toward other people.

On Serinda's Facebook page, I saw she was raising money through a bike ride across Cambodia for the Somaly Mam Foundation, which sought to end human trafficking and sex slavery. Instantly, I was interested in this cause. I sent Serinda a private message on Facebook, asking her for more information about what the bike ride entailed and how I could be of service to help make a difference.

After I did some research that day and evening on

Somaly Man's story, I knew I wanted to be a voice for this cause. Somaly Mam was fighting against a dark underworld industry that used girls as young as three as money-making tools. I knew brothels and prostitution were widespread in this part of the world. But the magnitude of it shocked me as I read the horrible facts. Human trafficking is the third largest organized crime in the world, and it is especially prevalent in Southeast Asia. The numbers are astounding—it is estimated that every year 2-4 million women and children are sold into prostitution. Most people turn a blind eye to such horrible crimes, but thinking of another human being with a heartbeat and feelings being sold, raped, abused, and tortured disturbed me in a way I never knew I could feel. So I began to ask myself: What if I could show the positive aspects of this cause? What if I could ride across Cambodia and capture some of the good coming from caring hearts like those of Somaly Mam and the other people who were fighting for this crime to be eradicated?

My trip to Southeast Asia was now taking on a new dimension. If Serinda got back to me the next day and the ride sounded like I thought it would, I would make the needed sacrifices to raise some money in the next few weeks before it began. Bali could wait! This would be my chance to raise awareness for this cause to the masses. I didn't want to intrude on the bike ride with my one man camera crew, but if I explained the *Return to Happiness* mission to all the riders and the people in charge of the foundation, I felt I could earn their blessings.

I woke up really early the next morning, thinking of our possible change of plan. I loved Cambodia and had been there a few years earlier. When I rolled over and checked my computer, I was elated to see that Serinda had made a prompt response. She left her number in Los Angeles so I could call her. I tried to go back to sleep, but the prospects of this ride fueled my thoughts and I became restless. When I did the math, I realized it was mid-day in the States. So I wandered out into the middle of the silent street outside our guesthouse and made the call.

Serinda was as bubbly as ever and sounded really happy to hear my voice. She said it was funny to hear from me. "I was just talking about you the other day, Ryan! I was telling a friend that I knew a guy who was involved in the game, and he was a really nice guy, and that nice guy was you!" "I'm honored," I replied with a laugh, but I also told her that my involvement in the game was now in the past, and I stood instead for what I could give to the world, not take! Serinda listened intently to my story of how I desired to make a positive change in the lives of others by never accepting failure, and she agreed I had made the right decisions. We were both Cancers, born in July, so on some deep level, I felt this call was no mere accident! I told her I would discuss going on the bike ride with Khalil and call her back in a few hours. I couldn't sleep so I banged on Khalil's door at 6 a.m. He was half-asleep, so I sat on the edge of the bed and stuttered a few words as I told him how excited I was about my conversation with Serinda. "Okay, okay," he said. Then we looked at each other intensely and said, "Let's do this!"

I called Serinda back after breakfast. I was multitasking, playing soccer with some kids while talking on the phone. She could hear the children in the background, and I was breathing a tad heavily to keep up with them. "Awww, oh my God, so cute," she said. Serinda loved kids and I knew she felt what I felt for the people over here. It was a beautiful, peaceful country, and I wanted to do my best to remove the bad from it. So I told Serinda I was in!

I didn't have much time to raise money since I had signed up for the bike ride so late and it was only two weeks away. A world donation page had been set up at the fundraising site www.Crowdrise.com for the ride, so I began talking about it with my family and friends online, sending out requests for donations through Facebook and other social media. After they understood the ride's purpose, people opened their kind hearts and donated directly on a page set up for me.

Meanwhile, Khalil and I bought tickets that same day to Siem Reap, Cambodia. The last evening in Laos before taking off to Siem Reap, I ventured down to the Mekong River. A group of merry men and some kids were laughing and yelling as they played a game called "7." The goal was to get these small clay balls as close to the main ball thirty feet down a dirt runway. I took the time to bond with the two teams of locals, who were sipping away on homemade liquor. They begged me to join in on the drinks, but I had to refrain. When I nailed the faraway ball on the first try, the locals all shook their heads and swarmed me with high-fives. The sun was just starting to set. Many of their kids just ran free along the riverbanks. They didn't stray far from the game, though, and I could tell what close family bonds these people shared. One little one in particular kept running into my arms for hugs. This kid was such a gem and loved throwing up the peace sign every time the camera was pointed in his direction.

We said our goodbyes and made our way back to the guesthouse where Marie and Alexandra were waiting to bid us farewell. We'd had some really good times with the girls and learned a lot about the temples, the monk rituals, and, of course, the mystic waterfalls and the nature that surrounded this small town. The girls had another four months of travel ahead of them, and in a way, I was envious of them.

I cherished all I had learned in Laos, I felt more connected than ever to the universal mind, infinite intelligence, God force, source energy, or whatever you may choose to call it. Khalil and I were creating our dream with unlimited resources at our disposal. Surprise after surprise fell into our laps, and for a cameraman, it was heaven on earth. Whenever I saw something of value that could be captured, I jumped at the opportunity. But now, Cambodia was going to be different. The last thing we wanted to do was interfere because of the sensitive nature of the trip. But we hoped we could help in this ride for a worthy cause.

CHAPTER 11
SIEM REAP, CAMBODIA

Flights were becoming second nature to Khalil and I now, so the quick jump to Siem Reap was easy. We had eleven days until before the ride, so we were going to spend at least a week in Siem Reap and then take a riverboat down the mighty Mekong. In Siem Reap, I went all out and got us a really nice hotel for $65 a night. I figured we had been semi-roughing it, so we needed a nice pool and room service. We planted down in Siem Reap, and the first day there, I got food poisoning from some fish I ate that I bought at the market. Good thing by this point that Khalil was like a parent to me. I was in agony while being sick out of both ends. If you ever visit Cambodia, watch the shady night markets; make sure they are clean, and most of all, get your shots. I had gotten my shots this time around, but I still got a bug. Oh well, I always say you have to accept a little bit of bad to experience so much good. Our diet the rest of that week consisted of pizzas and French fries at a groovy rooftop restaurant called the Red Piano. It had a cool picture of Angelina Jolie with the local owners taken back in 2000 when she was there filming *Tomb Raider*.

The Cambodian people, who are mainly devout Buddhists, are wonderful. Their country has been through a lot. For those unfamiliar with Cambodia's history, let me elaborate for a moment.

In the late 1970s, the kingdom of Cambodia came under rule by a dictator named Pol Pot, who could easily be compared to Hitler. He created strict rules for everyone in the country, and people who didn't obey would meet an untimely death. Because he was fearful that educated and wealthy people would overthrow him, he forced Cambodian youths to ravage through villages, loading trucks full of innocent people to be taken to concentration camps, such as Security Prison 21 (S-21), to be tortured. Then they were taken to the Killing Fields where they would be murdered and their corpses thrown into mass graves they first had to dig for themselves. Ultimately, it became a massive genocide that resulted in the killing of more than two million people. What a heinous crime! Pol Pot's reign of terror continued until his government collapsed in 1979.

Because of Pol Pot's crimes and murders, everyone in Cambodia today seems so young. The gruesome past is still very fresh in the Cambodians' minds. I had the privilege of meeting a man who had barely escaped death while he was chained by his ankles onto the floor in a small 4'x6' brick cell. He told me how he had been days away from being led to the Killing Fields. Because Cambodia's economy still suffers today, S-21 and the Killing Fields have been preserved in their original state to attract tourism. I had to see them. I had to educate myself on the atrocities. This time period had been filled with Cambodians killing Cambodians. I found it hard to believe this part of Cambodia's dark history, considering how kind were most of the people I met.

Our time spent in Siem Reap was awesome and very educational. I was put into contact with a tour guide named Adam Martin who would be in charge of our bike tour across Cambodia. We wanted to tell him about our project and get some insight on the rules and regulations of filming some of the sacred temples at Angkor Wat and the shelters we would be visiting. Adam and I took an instant liking to each other; he had a great sense of humor and a very pleasing personality. He was from Australia, but he had been based out of Saigon for the past few years. I knew that with him as our main guide on the trip, many laughs were going to be shared.

Adam was so kind that he put us in contact with a professional guide named Borin, who would take us to the sacred temple complex of Angkor Wat and tell us of the ancient Khmer civilization that had built it. Borin was very educated on the culture of Cambodia and went out of his way to take us to the main gate of the sacred temple the first day we met. He was at our hotel at 5 a.m. to meet us. He wanted to make sure we saw the sunrise in a perfect spot that wasn't too crowded. We took a tuk-tuk there in the pitch dark and grabbed some very strong coffee and baguettes to eat along the way.

When we arrived, what a gift it was to see the sun come over the massive temple! Angkor Wat has been called the eighth wonder of the world, and it's a major attraction that people come to see from all over the globe. This magnificent Hindu temple complex was built in the twelfth century as the king's state temple and capital at the heart of what had once been a thriving and immense city during the period the West calls the Middle Ages. In the late thirteenth century, it became a Buddhist temple, and today, it remains the world's largest religious monument. It is built out of sandstone with giant carved limestone lotus flowers. Everywhere, monks and elephants are scattered among the temple grounds, which are about the same size as

Manhattan.

After exploring the temples and meeting many people from around the world, Borin wanted to take us outside the city to a fishing village. The village was amazing! All the houses were on stilts for when the monsoon season came. Little rivers ran through the village with houses along their banks. All these rivers emptied out into the Tonlé Sap, Cambodia's major lake and river system.

We walked through the villages and met many locals. Borin told us there was only one television set in the entire village. We came across the TV and found fifty locals watching it intently on the roadside, and they didn't mind a bit as I sat in the dirt and joined them. They soon wondered who was the tattooed man from Canada who was making friends with them through the universal language of love. And everywhere, the children seemed attracted to me. Helen had been right—this trip more than anything was about the kids. I was beginning to see the full significance of this trip unfolding through what these kids were giving me. I was gaining more wisdom, yes! But more than anything else, I was rediscovering my inner child through these kids who radiated happiness and love despite their poverty.

An old monastery was our next stop along the way. When we arrived there, I stood outside the monastery and looked in amazement at its art work. Thank God we had Borin with us as our interpreter because right away a young monk came out and started talking to us. He grabbed me by the arm and led me inside the monastery. I looked at Borin and asked him what was going on. Borin said that the young monk had seen my Buddha necklace; I knew there had been something special about it; I could feel it. It was obvious because it caught the attention of locals and monks everywhere I went. KoKo had given it to me a few years earlier to show his respect for me, and at that time, he had told me that the necklace was over a century old and held much power.

Smiling, the monk took me to the back of the monastery where he slept. He introduced me to the headmaster, who must have been in his late eighties. Incense was lit and the two monks started to laugh with each other. They said a few things to Borin, who laughed as well. Then, still smiling, the young monk handed me an orange robe, and Borin told me that they wanted me to put it on! I was honored and immediately felt this was an experience I wouldn't pass up for the world. The young monk helped me put the robe on perfectly, so I was turned into a monk for a short time. Khalil was outside, still taking it all in, so I walked proudly outside the monastery, knowing I would give Khalil a shock. When he saw me, he shook his head and said, "Wow, are you kidding me, Ryan?" It was becoming the norm for those words to come out of his mouth. He took some really cool pictures of my new monk friends and me towering over them. What a blessing that we had been led here! It was another beautiful moment to remember. I respected these monks at the highest level for inviting me into their place of worship and letting me be a part of it. Out of respect, we did not want to film in their home, so I undressed and put on my civilian clothes to prepare to depart.

Before I left, however, Borin said the elder monk wanted to bless me. Feeling humbled, I knelt down on the ground. The monk lit more incense and started to pray while looking into my eyes. He started tapping my wrist that bore the bracelet from the old monk in Phuket. He then stared at me very intensely and started tapping the Buddha around my neck. I could feel the energy permeating from his thoughts. I had goose bumps all over. I obviously couldn't understand a word he said to me, but afterwards, Borin said the monk could sense that I was witnessing the great mysteries of life unfold on this journey. He blessed my soul for life after death and protection against accidents. He also said I would be a teacher to people everywhere that happiness is always easily accessible in the moment. Borin said the monk could feel that I had been weighed down by materialism and a closed mind in the past. But now I had let that go, and it was my duty to carry a message that while people are attached to "things," they need only to look inside themselves to find the peace that everyone deserves. I hugged both the monks and we got back onto our riverboat and found a place to eat on the water. And no kidding, I nailed my head again.

We went back to the grounds of Angkor Wat where a massive yellow balloon was taking people hundreds of feet into the air so they could see all the temples. We made the last ride to witness the sunset. It was only fitting. We had a heck of a time keeping our balance on the balloon as it swayed back and forth in the strong wind, though it was safely connected to a steel cable. We were a tad nervous that the cable would break, and a lot of other tourists had scared looks on their faces. But we made it! And the view was amazing! It was truly an amazing day! We also got the chance to feed and play with monkeys that day. I joked how Khalil had a lot in common with them. Strangely, we both did! In a good way, of course. The monkeys loved to play, and so did we. The food poisoning and any minor setbacks on the trip of a lifetime just made us more driven to take our lives and the project to the next level. To me, this trip was all about connecting with the local people wherever we went.

We planned to visit Siem Reap again after our bike ride, but now we were off to Phnom Penh, Cambodia's capital. To get there, we had to take a riverboat, which resembled a plane fuselage cut in half, down the mighty Mekong River. We passed many villages along the way and so many people waved at us. Once we arrived at the port, we saw hundreds of tuk-tuk and cab drivers who wanted to take the boat passengers to hotels, hostels, or other accommodations.

That morning before we got onto the boat, however, an older lady had arranged for a van to pick us up at the port and bring us into the city. The van was so crammed with about fifteen passengers that I was lucky to get the front seat. When I grabbed my luggage upon our arrival in Phnom Penh, a kind man came directly up to me and said, "I was sent from God to be your guide my friend! My name is Curly." It was a bold statement, but something in his eyes told me he was sincere and authentic. So my intuition told me he would be our guide. He tried to carry all our bags, and jovially said, "Just relax; you are my guests, and welcome to Phnom Penh, Cambodia!" I laughed and felt very at ease with Curly as another friendship developed instantly.

CHAPTER 12
PHNOM PENH, CAMBODIA

Wow, Phnom Penh was buzzing. When I told Curly we wanted to visit a local orphanage, he said he knew the perfect one for us to spread some love. When I asked him what the orphanage needed the most, he looked at me and said, "Mr. Ryan, they be so happy if we deliver some big bags of rice." I was excited. And I trusted Curly. He was a wise man who told us about all the issues from his country's past and how hard it was to make a living there, but he was still happy because he got to show Phnom Penh and its outlying areas to visitors from all over the world. I took Curly out for lunch, and then he helped us to find a hotel that just happened to be right beside the hotel we would be staying at and from where the bike ride would leave. I gave Curly the funds to get the rice, and he promised to be outside our hotel at nine the next morning so we could go see the orphaned kids. My thoughts were right. Curly slept out of his tuk-tuk. He told me the next day that he was from a small village three hours outside the capital city.

When we stepped out of the hotel the next morning, he had the two bags of rice and said, "Good morning" with a giant smile.

The orphanage was about a half hour away, and Curly's spirit added enthusiasm to the ride. When we reached the orphanage, Curly drove the tuk-tuk right into the yard while all the kids jumped in, swarming us with love. I got out and ran behind the tuk-tuk with two youngsters in my arms while Curly kept yelling, "We got the rice!" These kids were so happy, and I was very grateful that Curly had gone out of his way to help without any idea how much I would pay him at the end of our journey to make this all happen.

We were told by the people who ran the local orphanage that these big bags of rice would keep the kids fed for over three months. That was a very warm feeling. We started playing basketball with all these precious children on sand with an old tattered basketball hoop. We danced and laughed. Then we were shown the living quarters, which were very rough. Up to six kids lived in a small room with bunk beds. The kids loved the sound gear when Khalil placed his headphones on one of the youngster's ears. That kid then shared them with his friends.

One five-year old boy, who had undergone heart surgery the previous year, had a spirit that really stood out. He was so full of energy, and when it was time to leave, he grabbed my arm and didn't want to let go. Again, as in Khao Lak, I wished we could have stayed longer, but we only had so much time. Just that we'd had the chance to give these children who had no parents some hope and love is what mattered the most. And not one of them was in a state of sadness! Every one of them laughed and joked with us. Some of the kids were as old as sixteen, and the people who ran the orphanage told us they now had very slim chances of ever having a real family. Of course, Khalil and I shared sad emotions that day, but the kids made us feel better by their laughter and smiles. It was as if everything were okay and they wanted us to feel good.

After the visit, Khalil wanted to see the Killing Fields and S-21 concentration camp. I could tell Curly wasn't excited about going to these places, but Khalil had to see them. I had seen them a few years previously and they had made me sick. How twisted Pol Pot had been to have so many innocent people murdered for no reason at all. At the entrance of the Killing Fields was a mass grave with thousands of skulls and bones; people who had been maimed by landmines were there, playing music for donations. The energy here was dark. So many innocent people killed for no reason. I was sick and so was Curly. He didn't even want to step into the grounds, but Khalil hadn't been there and wanted to see them. I made sure our visit there wasn't very long. There were teeth from the dead, and old clothes and bones that rose to the surface during the rainy season. It was a hot day, and after the visit to the orphanage, it made me really sad. I thought of all the families and what it must have been like in the streets and villages during the time of this genocide. Babies had even been killed against trees. This wasn't happiness at all, so after half an hour, I had to get away from there and I refused to film anything.

After a quick lunch, we visited S-21, a concentration camp with strict rules for imprisoned Cambodians who were captured by the Khmer Rouge. It saddened me to see how this place had been run. Prisoners had been brought here and tortured. If they showed the slightest bit of resistance against the hierarchy, they would be tortured in inhumane ways, including through terrible beatings and electrocution. Because the atrocities committed here are so fresh in the minds of Cambodians and the world, the structure still stands untouched. The rooms are unchanged and even the beds people were shackled to remain the same. Pictures of the dead cover the walls. And the faces of so many innocent people no longer with us cover the walls of the Cambodian people's memories. Curly and I just shook our heads in disgust. I could tell he was ashamed to think this type of thing had happened in his country. I could feel the negative energy surrounding the camp and thought perhaps the spirits of the deceased lingered in its energy field. Whatever the case, I wanted to remember this day for the love we gave and received from the kids, so we did not stay long.

Now it was off to Grasshopper Bike Shop, where Adam had suggested I load up on my biking gear for the big trip across the country. Raw Travel, whose staff would be our guides across Cambodia, worked in conjunction with Grasshopper for the bike race. The staff at Grasshopper was awesome! As soon as I walked in, they were full of enthusiasm. I was given some fresh, ice cold coconut water, straight from the coconut—by far my favorite drink. We joked and laughed as I tried on different shorts, playing around like I was a model. They told me I reminded them of Adam Martin, which I gratefully took as a compliment since I held Adam in high regard. I picked out my first pair of spandex ever (I had previously sworn I would never sport them), but comfort was going to be very important on this long journey. Finally, I was decked out in florescent yellow, black, and white shorts and a killer biking t-shirt that went well with the Grasshopper colors.

Next, I needed a haircut, so I found a great little barbershop nearby. I swear I got the best haircut of my life there, and for only three American dollars, but I gave the kind man five bucks and told him to keep the change. He got a kick out of my antics when I held a fan over my head as a makeshift blow dryer while he trimmed away. He laughed his butt off, and so did the other guys working at the salon. They all laughed at me as I grabbed a big fan to cool myself down on this very hot day.

It was funny how I now just laughed at life and the experiences I moved through. My life was so different now from any experiences I'd had previously, whether while playing hockey, partying, or drug dealing. Now I knew that each and every one of us is on a path, and my path was illuminated by shining lights like I'd never felt before. I felt I was in the never-ending flow of meeting great people who were all aligned for the purpose of teaching me what everything is about in life.

That night I took a trip down to the Mekong River to break in my new biking gear. Khalil and I thought my walking around in my new uniform would get some people laughing. We giggled like kids when I put it on because I looked like some overgrown Tour de France competitor. I didn't feel like much of a competitor—I figured the other riders who would be on the trip had been training intensely for it, so I felt a tad nervous.

After throwing around a ball with some kids and stretching out my body with some locals on the boardwalk, I was approached by a man of short stature dressed in fitness apparel. He asked me in broken English if I would help him lead an outdoor aerobics class. I could tell from how he looked at me that he thought I stuck out like a sore thumb in this place, but he could also tell that I put a lot of energy into maintaining my physical body. I agreed to help, and I high-fived the majority of the students, whom I later found out came on a daily basis to get their workouts. I found it tough to synchronize my moves with my fellow instructor as dance music played. I smiled even though I had to do my best to stay focused. The class attracted many onlookers and stopped a lot of traffic—must have been my spandex. I worked up a good sweat and saw that Khalil was having a hard time holding the camera because he was laughing so hard.

When the class was over, I shook my head and said, "Time for a shower!" Then we made our way back to the hotel, put the camera away, and went out on the town for a nice dinner. While we ate, we talked about what the next few days might be like. We were both filled with enthusiasm and gratitude for everything that we'd seen and put into action thus far.

The following morning, I bid farewell to my new friend Curly, whom it seemed I had known for many years now. I knew all about his family and his values. He had taught me a lot about Cambodia's history and about my own character. I could see myself in him despite how we had grown up in different countries; the openness in our hearts made us connect on a soul level that would last for infinity. When I walked out of the hotel, there was Curly with his smile and the same plaid shirt and jeans he'd been wearing since our first meeting a few days previously. He told me he was heading back to his small village to see his family. Then he told me he didn't want any money! This response caught me off-guard, but Curly told me that he loved happiness and seeing people in a state of joy. "Ryan, I believe in *Return to Happiness*, and my happiness to you is I don't want to accept your money."

Little did Curly know at the time that I had five hundred American dollars I wanted to give him. I knew that would help his family live comfortably for a long time. After hearing him out and seeing tears well up in his eyes, I grabbed Curly's left hand and placed the money in it. I told him, "Curly, you are a true friend and your going the extra mile has not gone unnoticed. Not once have you asked for a thing, so please take this money and buy something nice for your wife and kids." We then had a warm embrace without either of us saying a word. We just looked at each other and felt what the other felt from deep down inside.

As I was walking away, a man in his sixties approached and demanded that Curly drive him to the airport. "Five dollars, get me to the airport!" he barked. I turned back, looked the man in the eyes, and said, "Sir, the man who is taking you to the airport right now is one of the most authentic men I've ever met; please take the kindness in your heart and give him twenty dollars." The man calmed down and switched his demeanor since he could see the emotion in my eyes, so he said, "Okay!" He actually shook my hand. I then walked away, and simultaneously, Curly and I gave each other the thumbs up as he drove away. That proved to me that Curly was like family to me, and no matter what race we each came from, we were bonded simply by sharing this planet together.

CHAPTER 13
THE RIDE AND GIVING BACK

"Service to others is the rent you pay for your room here on earth."
— Mohammad Ali

The evening before the ride, all the participants got briefed on the journey we were about to embark on. Twenty people would ride, all with one goal in mind, to make a positive change for the better. Some of my readers may wonder how human trafficking and sex slavery are relevant to my quest for happiness. I've learned that finding long-lasting peace and happiness in many instances comes through pain and suffering. And all the people I was about to meet—the riders, the girls, and Somaly Mam—were living proof of change in the right direction. It didn't matter where we came from in the world; we quickly bonded because we had come together to ride for the purpose of making a positive difference in the lives of people who needed our help.

When I saw Serinda in the elevator, she looked great. She was now one of the stars of the television show

Breakout Kings, a season of which she had just finished filming. I felt a lot of respect for her that she had come all the way from Los Angeles to ride for this cause. When all the riders introduced themselves and gave their reasons for participating, she said how she felt at peace being here because the Hollywood lifestyle could be so very competitive and overwhelming. Where we were now, people didn't judge you so much on your appearance or what you had in terms of material possessions. We were a group of twenty riders all with the same intent—to give back! Unlike those I rode for, I had never been raped or tortured, but I knew what it was like to live in a cage. I knew what it was like to feel alone. Everything I had experienced in life up to this point gave me a deeper understanding and empathy for how others felt inside who were hurting.

All the riders were told that physical preparation was necessary; we would be in the saddle up to seven hours per day for successive days. A fitness program was recommended to everyone involved. Khalil and I were last minute additions, so thank God we were in good shape.

I wanted to educate myself as much as possible on the cause for which I was riding. Who was Somaly Mam? What did she stand for? And what adversities had she surmounted to achieve the kind of success that is capable of saving lives. On Wikipedia, I read about her life—how she had conceived the first center for girls so she could give them a real life and teach them life skills so once they were rehabilitated, they would be ready to enter the world as human beings and not commodities for sale! The team I was riding with was about to see Somaly's work in action—the tangible results of what others can do to help people who suffer.

In my research into Somaly's life, I learned that she had been an orphan until a man she came to call her "grandfather" picked her up and made her into his slave.

Then when she was fourteen, her "grandfather" sold her into a brothel. For the next ten years, her life was one of severe suffering. She was abused, raped, and, of course, saw horrifying acts of unspeakable deeds done to others that would haunt her for the rest of her life. Eventually, she was forced into marriage with a man who abused her and forced her to prostitute herself, having sex with five or six men a day.

In her early twenties, Somaly Mam managed to escape from this lifestyle and leave Cambodia with the help of a French aid worker. Later, I read in Somaly's riveting book *The Road to Lost Innocence* how hard she found it to forget her past and leave behind the other girls who had been in the same situation as herself. As a result, Somaly became a brave leader and advocate in the fight against sex slavery and human trafficking. She made it her purpose to rescue young women who were forced to work in the sex trade against their will—some as young as two years old. Through her efforts, over 7,000 young women have been rescued from sex slavery and rehabilitated. Somaly was inspired by her own personal adversities to give these girls unconditional love and help them through the healing process, eventually reintegrating them back into society and giving them a new life. Somaly Mam exemplifies courage and strength, and she represents how just one person's faith and action can bring about so much change in the world.

I quickly realized that the majority of the riders on this mission had also gone through their own adversities. On the first day of the ride, I was very blessed to meet a kind and gentle soul by the name of Terry Enright. Terry had prostate cancer and had lost his wife a few years earlier. I was drawn to Terry immediately and knew just like everyone else I'd met in life that it was for a reason. I saw myself in Terry, despite our thirty-five-year age gap. Terry was passionate about helping others, and he talked in-depth about how he had lost many friends in the Vietnam War.

He was pure love in the broadest sense. He told me how his wife had given a life full of love and that he held her spirit close to his heart.

Terry didn't let on to any of the riders how much he was suffering. We traversed along a dusty dirt road that first day, and Terry took a nasty spill right beside me. He banged his knee up pretty badly and cut his elbow. But he bounced up like a kid and shook it off like nothing had happened at all, stating, "It's going to take more than a little fall to hold me up from what I believe in!" Terry was bandaged up by our group leader, a thirty-year-old gentleman from Siem Reap named Cham. Cham was proud of his country and even more proud of the cause we were riding for. Most people would have packed it in for the day, but Terry pushed on like a true warrior. And that's what I called Terry, a warrior of life who walked the walk of giving back, wearing his heart on his sleeve at all times. He didn't live his life in a half-ass way—he was a doer.

For Terry, it was all about the kids who needed saving. Terry told me he was in Cambodia to open up a school he had funded in memory of his late wife. The day after the ride was over, he had to go to the school for the opening and to see the kids he was providing with the chance for a better life through education. Terry had such passion and he was so driven by doing good that, in my mind, he became the biggest inspiration in our group. Inspiration isn't just a word! It's a feeling that drives many human beings to do better for themselves and the world. Terry defined the word in its truest sense.

Day 1: Tom Dy Rehabilitation Center

That first day, we rode to the Tom Dy Centre in Phnom Penh where we got to meet a great group of women "survivors" of sex trafficking. The center was built in 2004 and has the capacity to shelter sixty women. It offers basic reading, math, and life skills courses, as well as vocational training with the aim of assisting residents to find sustainable employment and gain economic sufficiency. The women we met there were part of Voices for Change. Modeled after Somaly Mam's life and experience, Voices for Change is a program that gives survivors of sex trafficking a voice in their lives by helping them to educate the public on the nature of sex trafficking and human slavery.

We had a great lunch with the women and saw firsthand what Somaly's hard work and perseverance had done to give hope to a fight that seemed like an uphill battle. Before our lunch with the girls, a very energetic personality stood up to share her story. Her name was Shrey Pek. Trafficked at the age of seven, she is now a brave leader working in the advocacy department of the Somaly Mam Foundation. She was surrounded by her friends and fellow survivors while she gave her tearful story of what had happened in her early life. After being floored by the tragic past of physical and emotional harm that was inflicted on her, we all came together as a group to share many hugs and laughs. The girls who worked for Voices for Change knew why we were riding, and I could tell they had the highest respect for our willingness to give back in any way we could.

Until that day, I had known little about the organized crime of human trafficking, and I sure wasn't prepared for what I heard. Also at that lunch, I met a girl named Samana, who was missing an eye. She really caught my attention because even though she was brutally beaten and her eye gouged out with a spoon, she had refused to service clients due to her pain. The scars on her face from her punishment would last forever. Regardless, she and all the girls glowed with love. I could tell that they had forgiven any wrongdoing that had ever happened to them. Now they actually went to the brothels to hand out condoms and give hope to others.

That first day was a great testament to Somaly's work to

make a difference in the lives of girls who had been through so much. I know it's hard to think about, but just imagine being a young girl sold into a brothel—and in many cases, by a member of your own family! It's sick, twisted, and inconceivable in my mind. But the survivors are pillars of strength who make this cause all the more powerful. They make it clear that the rape and abuse of any human being needs to be stopped. And it's people like you and me who can have such a profound impact by giving positive attention to the people who need our help.

After lunch, we all rode on with new energy and a deeper understanding of why we were doing what we were. That first day of riding was mostly about getting accustomed to our new bikes, the task at hand, and, of course, our new family. Adventure was in our hearts, and the factual stories of the girls drove us to move forward and be present in the moment. Not one rider complained about the heat or the intense road conditions we were experiencing. That first day, the warm up to our emotions and stamina gave us just a taste of the days ahead.

Day 2: Phnom Penh to Sihanoukville

The second day of the ride was hot, to say the least, but we were excited to be riding approximately eighty kilometers to the beautiful port city of Sihanoukville. I had never in my life ridden that far on a bike in one day. Raw Travel had everything very organized. A van rode ahead of us and another behind. Inside the vans was sufficient fruit and water to keep us well-hydrated. We would stop every twenty or so kilometers for a break. We left really early that day because we had to transfer out of Phnom Penh to begin our ride south through the countryside and to the coast. We were riding through rural Cambodia, passing timeless scenes of water buffalo and rice paddies. In the distance, we could see the Cardamom Mountains, one of the country's last wild places. We were becoming quickly accustomed to the mountain bikes. The riding through the Cambodian cities, towns, and on dirt roads made me feel free and able to soak up the beauty. Kids were running up to greet us with endless smiles and love. It saddened me to know that one in forty of these girls would be sold into the business of sex slavery. I saw what we were riding for—the generations of the future—and how necessary it was for us to stand up for what was right.

Day 3: Sihanoukville to Kampot

By the third day, the team had really bonded. We had let down all our inhibitions. We were telling each other a lot of deep and profound experiences from our lives. We had become like a family, sharing this journey together. We rode 104 kilometers that day from Sihanoukville to Kampot. It was a challenging ride that demanded a lot of physical and mental strength, but we all rooted each other on with Cham always in the lead. We rode within sight of the Cambodian coastline, and by afternoon, the roads were flat and under the shadow of the Elephant Mountains. Early that evening, we arrived in Kampot, a sleepy provincial center built on the banks of a river and full of displaced French architecture. We were tired and wet with perspiration, but checking into the hotel was like a breath of fresh air. Exhausted, I flopped down on my bed before I took a cold shower. Everyone in the group looked proud and accomplished. We were having fun, getting in better shape, and most importantly, on a mission.

Day 4: Kep-sur-Mer and Rabbit Island

After a pleasant and short thirty-kilometer ride in the morning, we reached the beachside town of Kep-sur-Mer, an old French colonial resort that has found a new lease on life and is a popular weekend destination with visitors from Phnom Penh. Here we took a boat to the secluded, small Rabbit Island over crystal clear water. The sun was hot and the whole group was excited to get some downtime.

Rabbit Island is only two square kilometers in size, and the boat ride was only twenty-five minutes. A bunch of us dove in about a hundred meters from the shore and swam in the warm water. Starfish were everywhere; sea turtles would swim up to the surface, and the tropical fish were beautiful and abundant. The moment we got there, I enjoyed at least three cold coconuts. I had another jump in the sea and then rested in a nearby hammock to soak in this precious moment of time. I learned that only about six or seven families lived on the island; of course, they had a restaurant and cooked us a wonderful authentic Cambodian meal. They made their living fishing and growing coconut trees. When I held one of their newborn babies, I once again gave thanks for the expansion of goodness flowing into my life.

Despite our fun in the sun, when we got back to port, some of us had some serious sunburns. The Asian sun doesn't mess around. Since I was looking red, after talking and shaking hands with a group of about twenty monks, I was in much need of some aloe vera.

Day 5: Ride/Transfer to Phnom Penh

This day we got an early start on our ninety kilometers to be spent riding on Cambodian highways. Our route took us north, away from the coast and back toward Phnom Penh. We passed through the provincial town of Takeo. Then when we got close to Phnom Penh, we boarded the vans and drove into the city to avoid the traffic. We enjoyed another night in the capital on the mighty Mekong, having a great meal together and reflecting on the long days and the locals we had met thus far, while enjoying our newfound friendships with one another.

We'd had a few minor falls on the road, but because our willingness to get this ride done was so strong, the pain didn't affect our passion or determination. One of the riders actually went down hard on the pavement in front of me. When I helped her up, she insisted she was fine. Only weeks later did I found out that this selfless woman, Phay Phamna, had a fracture. I had a few close calls myself, but thankfully, no serious wipeouts. My favorite time riding was when it cooled down in the evening and I could see the setting sun. Then the breeze was much cooler on our faces, and the conversation became more intimate as we discussed topics like what our lives had been like growing up and how we had all ended up together on this ride for hope.

Day 6: Kampong Cham to Phnom Penh

This morning's route started from the town of Koh Kong where we started one of my favorite rides along the mighty Mekong River all the way to Kampong Cham. We found ourselves riding on unsealed roads through many villages. We heard music from temples, saw waving children lining the route, and shared the road with livestock. We arrived in the evening in Kampong Cham, Cambodia's second largest city, situated on the Mekong. We had cycled sixty-five kilometers that day.

Day 7: Kampong Cham to Beng Mealea

The next morning, we transferred out of Kampong Cham and rode through the countryside to the fabulous ruined temple of Beng Mealea, still overgrown with jungle vines and very atmospheric with few visitors. On the way to Siem Reap, we rode parallel to the Tonlé Sap, the largest freshwater lake in Southeast Asia. The lake's waters control the flow of the Mekong and provide a living for thousands of people since it is one of the world's richest sources of freshwater fish. After Beng Mealea, we boarded the vans again, which took us onward to the tourist mecca of Siem Reap, home of the famed Angkor Wat temple complex. We traversed eighty kilometers that day, and we all started to feel that the journey was nearing an end. We were proud of our mental and physical strength that kept us moving forward in pursuit of our goal. And meeting Somaly Mam was just around the corner at the AFESIP (translated from French as "Acting for Women in Disturbing Situations") shelter.

Day 8: Angkor Wat Temples and Ride to Banteay

On this day, we had an orientation ride around Angkor Wat's main temples, located about seven kilometers outside the city. Although I had visited it before, I still found this amazing and extensive world heritage site to be truly breathtaking in its beauty and scale. After this visit, we had the rest of the day off. Riding was becoming so much easier now that I was wishing this experience could last a month. That day we cycled thirty-five kilometers.

Day 9: AFESIP Shelter Visit in Siem Reap and Meeting Somaly Mam

This day was going to be one of the most profound and impactful days of my life. I was going to see some of Somaly's work in action. I was going to see many girls who had been recently saved, survivors who came from the Tom Dy Centre. I was about to see what the human heart can create through love and compassion.

To me, the eyes tell you a lot about a person; in my opinion, they are the windows to the soul. They can tell many stories of sadness, but also speak stories of love and courage. Let me tell you, on this day I willed myself to ride. I was sunburned in the face, had a migraine, and was having signs of vertigo. I was trying to stay as hydrated as possible, but the heat can get so intense, especially for a foreigner from the West. But I knew we were going to the AFESIP shelter that day. And I had a good feeling I was going to meet the person who was responsible for the creation of the Somaly Mam Foundation, an organization with such power because of Somaly and her global alliance's unconditional love and tireless work ethic. Over 7,000 people had survived this sick crime due in part to Somaly Mam's passion to help others and her risking her own life on countless occasions. Her mission is to save lives, and she does it with love. Her heart fills the interspaces of the universe.... And when I jumped off my bike when we finally arrived at the AFESIP center, Somaly ran to me like a young child.

I could feel her magnetic vibration and intensity as we wrapped arms in a beautiful embrace. She told me she recognized me from Facebook. I was honored that she knew a little about me and what I stood for. Her smile radiates pure love—you couldn't miss it—and she has no hatred in her heart. One of her main messages is to forgive the people who have wronged us, not to hate people, and, of course, that everybody's role is so important. I could tell that each girl who had been rescued looked up to Somaly like she was her mom. Maybe "Mam" in some ways stood for "Mom." Whatever the case, she made time for everyone that day. People really admire Somaly, and she's been recognized as one of the 100 most influential people in the world. She speaks all over the world, expressing her belief that no child, no person, should be treated with such abuse. I had tears in my eyes when I met Somaly, and so did she. It made me see her humanity. When I looked into her eyes, all I could see was love and purpose.

She had earned my respect! And for her to take the time to be on film for me gave me so much gratitude for the force that had allowed me to become involved with one of the world's most serious global issues. Somaly told me what made her happy. "What makes me happy is when I see my kids graduate law school." And she told me how proud she was to see the transmutation take place from their being victims to surviving and thriving. She told me that all the girls who had been rescued from the brothels were her heroes. "Those are my heroes; they are my heroes!" While for me every day is special, this one will be imprinted deep in my soul forever. I was so honored to meet someone with such drive for saving others. Imagine if we all had just ten percent of the desire and drive Somaly has, what a different world it would be.

Somaly immediately set about playing host to us. She had the young girls perform a traditional Cambodian dance; they had all been working hard on it so they could make the right moves. And it moved people to see it—to see the results we were all riding for. Somaly cooked for us that day; she made us feel welcome. And then she had to get back to work. Her work is what she loves, although it comes with risks. Somaly was placed on this earth to teach people that no matter where you come from, your dreams and your never-give-up attitude have the power to transform the world. She is well-known, but she didn't begin her mission to become famous. The fame came because she spoke up loudly and proudly for the people she wanted to help.

Our group listened to a lot of stories from young girls who had been raped and tortured. Somaly obviously needed us to hear the girls. One of the young girls spoke with an interpreter, saying she was raped at the age of four. She had been warned that if she didn't do what she was told, she would be killed. Then she told the crowd, at least one hundred people deep, "I have a heart just like anyone else."

Tears flowed, and then we danced. It was tangible change in the right direction. I now had a deeper respect for all the work that goes into saving these girls. Human trafficking and sex slavery is a worldwide epidemic, but its surface is being scratched by people like Somaly, her girls, and now, of course, a global alliance that will keep pushing forward until one day human trafficking becomes a thing of the past. Future generations will benefit from the work we all do as a human nation today. And, of course, we benefit as well. The reality of the change lives inside the human heart.

Day 10: Angkor Wat

Angkor Wat is where we finished off the 500km ride of our lives. It was only fitting that we experienced the sunrise there as a group. I gazed around the sacred site and saw that the people I'd made bonds with soon would be back in their respective cities, working their jobs away from the dirt roads, small beach town hotels, and centers where we had shared openly such emotional experiences. I'm sure I speak on behalf of all the riders when I say that none of our lives have been the same since that ride. We saw so much beauty and change on this mission. Leaving Cambodia was going to be tough, but knowing the team I rode with raised $122,000 for the Somaly Mam Foundation made it so worthwhile. Everything truly is temporary, but knowing that so many lives are being changed gave me and all the others a sense of accomplishment. What I learned through just listening to others' personal journeys while riding, at dinner, or in hotel lobbies and rooms gave me a personal memory bank to draw on forever. We took a nice photo together that night at a local restaurant in Siem Reap; it is a testament to all the riders that we stuck together, made it fun, and not only found our own happiness but gave to others—that's what it was all about.

CHAPTER 14
CHIANG MAI—FREEDOM

"Freedom is not worth having if it does not include the freedom of making mistakes."
— Gandhi

Leaving Cambodia was harder than I had expected. The attachment I felt to the people of Cambodia, all the riders, the young girls whose lives were being changed and the ones who were still trapped in brothels was so very fresh in my mind. I never knew I could feel emotions like I was now feeling. Meeting Somaly was a moment I will never forget, and being able to call her my friend is something I cherish. How one woman's dream could be planted into the minds of so many was so powerful to see, and I was honored to be part of it. And little did I know what the next day would have in store for me.

Chiang Mai was to be the last stop on the *Return to Happiness* journey. Khalil and I arrived in Chiang Mai in the early evening. The city reminded me a lot of Bangkok because of the busy night markets. Khalil and I reflected on the bike ride at dinner, shared our sincere emotions with each other, and discussed what we had learned about the cause. It was a cause for which I wanted to be a voice forever. As we walked down the streets of Chiang Mai, it was hard to put everything we had been exposed to into perspective. The team of riders had become a family in a very short time. Now I had to return to my life in Canada, but I knew we had our work cut out for us in editing our film. We had been very selective with all the shots we took throughout the ride. But what stuck out the most was Somaly's message of unconditional love—how we can't hate people who have done wrong, no matter what—we should love people who make mistakes and forgive them.

Everything Somaly had said resonated in my heart. I knew that I had met all these like-minded people for a reason. I had learned even more about myself through hearing about their adversities and the bumps along their life paths. They taught me more about happiness because I learned about what meant the most in their lives—family, love, and giving.

My morning ritual was always the same—up early, turning my phone on, and checking my email. Usually, I received an inspirational message from my mom or dad. This particular morning would be one I will never forget. I was about to get some news that would round out the trip in such a manner that everything would make even more sense for me. I turned on my phone and saw that my dad had sent me an email entitled, "Good Things Happen To Good People." When I opened the email, I couldn't believe the words I read: "Today's a day that all our family can rejoice as you've been granted full access for business and for pleasure by the United States Department of Homeland Security." As I read, I broke down in tears of joy. I was shaking from being in such a state of shock and elation. Khalil jumped up and put the camera on me immediately. There was no hiding these emotions. He thought there was a death in the family until I read him the message that my dad had sent me. I couldn't contain myself as I ran around the room, jumping for joy! The first thing I did was call my dad and put the phone on speaker.

As tears ran down my face, my dad confirmed the good news for me, and he told me, "If there's the Law of Attraction, or whatever, everything is paying off. It's all worthwhile. Whatever you've been doing, it's the right thing. You know, you're doing good to the world. And good things happen to good people. I've said that to you since you were born, and now this has come back to pay huge dividends for you. And you will benefit so, so greatly on this. I mean, I think it's just absolutely—a test from somebody, wherever—I don't know, man. I mean, everybody is so excited for you. Just keep going the way you're going and pursue greatness—whatever that is, you just have to keep going for it, you know. Thank God for my family and thank God for friends, and thank God for good people around me, and thank God for a good cause."

After talking to my dad and hearing his affirmation of me, I felt so high on life. I called Sadie's mom next to tell her the news. We both screamed into the phone. It had happened! For years now, I had written down that I would be granted access to the country I had been told I would never be allowed back in. I had set up that vision in my mind and never stopped believing. I had written it down with emotion day after day for years and kept reaffirming to myself that it would happen. And now it had! And at the perfect time because now I actually deserved it. Thoughts truly do manifest into reality! It's what we think that matters the most.

Before I got off the phone with Sadie's mom, I asked her not to tell Sadie because I wanted to surprise my daughter. Already, I was envisioning showing up at her door unexpectedly and I could feel how excited she would be.

After pacing in the room at the downtown Chiang Mai Hotel, not knowing what to do with myself, it was time for Khalil and I to go out and celebrate in style. I was vibrating at such a positive frequency that I felt I was so much bigger than my mind, body, and soul. I was an infinite part of the whole of the universe, and nature had rewarded me now for my patience and acts of kindness. My daughter and my family would no longer have to suffer. Sadie and her mom would no longer have to make such great sacrifices so Sadie could come to visit me every summer. Now no borders would get in the way of my seeing my little girl. I had just received the ultimate gift. And my gratitude oozed out of me with every step I walked, hopped, and ran that day. Unlimited happiness and energy poured forth from my physical body.

Khalil and I now felt we were on an adventure. A giant Buddha statue stood at the top of the city so I wanted to visit it and give thanks to the power that had made it possible for my dream to crystallize into physical reality. First, I helped a lady along the roadside to cook up a dish of Pad Thai, a traditional Thai dish. She laughed away as I helped her. Next, I helped a bunch of men set up their vendor booths for the market that day. I had to keep giving back in every shape and form for the gift I had received that day. As I walked down a crowded street, I saw people playing music and joined in on the shows. I sported an Asian hat and smiled ear-to-ear. I said to Khalil, "People are looking at me like I'm nuts!" They were, but they were all full of smiles. God, I love making other people smile; it's so easy—just smile with genuine love and it always comes back! Plus, you make someone's day.

Finally, Khalil and I jumped into a taxi and the driver brought us to the base of the trail that led to the "Big Buddha" at the top of the city. The driver told us there were only two hundred stairs to the top and he agreed to accompany us up them. But he had miscalculated. That was okay, though. I just laughed at him and asked, "What are those? Fake steps. Here's the two hundred steps!" He waved his hat in front of his face and said in broken English, "I sooooo tired." I just took off like mad and sprinted to the top in excitement. It was worth it because the view at the top was breathtaking.

I met a lady at the top who was ninety-five years old—she could have fooled me. Her smile was like a ray of light. Seeing her smile made it crystal clear that as humans, we have won the greatest lottery, and that's the gift of life, to be alive on this planet. I lit some incense and gave thanks. Then I got into a discussion with a monk about the gift I had received that day. We talked about how all humans suffer in the physical world, but it's our duty to keep our minds closed tightly against negative subjects. He gave me strength, energy, and courage to keep on keeping on for the rest of my journey.

CHAPTER 15
HAPPINESS

"You are only as happy as you allow yourself to be."
— Abraham Lincoln

We were now going home. But I had one more leg to my journey. A few days after arriving in Vancouver, I was going to enter the U.S. I was now going to put final closure to my past mistakes by seeing my daughter in her hometown for the first time since she was a year old. For some reason, when I crossed the border at the Vancouver airport, it didn't seem like a miracle or shock. I had always believed it would happen one day, and I had never stopped writing it down in my journal like it had happened already. I had never stopped believing. Believing is the key to so many people's dreams coming true—the key to making it reality is to visualize what you want and know it is going to happen in a state of mind injected with so much faith that there is no other possibility but for it to happen. If you can really see it, and believe it, the universe has all the means to make it happen.

I flew alone to Wichita since Khalil had already returned to Montreal, but he was going to come to Wichita to capture my special moment on film. I had thought we were close to finishing the film, but as I flew to Wichita, I realized that *Return to Happiness* had only begun. This opportunity was going to open doors for me to live my purpose as a better father and humanitarian to all who needed my help.

Landing on U.S. soil in Wichita felt amazing to me. I had arranged to meet Sadie's mom and her boyfriend at a local pizza restaurant to help plan my surprise reunion with Sadie and capture it on film. I was really happy to see them. I knew my daughter was being raised by an awesome mom, and the boyfriend was a great role model with a daughter of his own. Sadie's mom's opinion of me meant a lot, and I had worked hard on my character over the years to prove to her that Sadie had a caring father who loved her. No matter the physical distance between us, I had proven I would always be there for her. I wanted to surprise Sadie and capture the moment on film. As I met with them, I was a bundle of nerves. Where had all the time gone? All my memories of hockey and Sadie's birth came rushing back into my mind. The past twelve years had taught me a lot about people and purpose, but most of all, I think those years had been God's way of teaching me humility, and, of course, gratitude.

We all discussed how Sadie's life was changing a lot these days. She wasn't a little girl anymore; she was growing into a young lady. Any father out there knows the feeling when he looks at his son or daughter and sees that they aren't just a little one anymore. The innocence of a child is so sacred, something that, in my humble opinion, we all need to hold onto. I just wanted to inject faith into my daughter that she could be anything in this world as long as she dreamed big and pursued what she loved with passion. "It's simple," I would always tell her over the phone.

"Whatever you do, always do your best, and most of all, have fun!"

Our much anticipated reunion was scheduled for the following afternoon. When I called for a taxi, an elderly gentleman named Curtis showed up outside the Marriot's Courtyard Hotel in downtown Wichita. He wore old worn jeans with suspenders, sported a cap, and had shoulder-length white hair and a beard to boot—he looked almost like Santa Claus and made the trip special for me. After all, I was as excited as a kid on Christmas morning that I would soon be surprising my daughter.

Khalil and I were to meet Sadie's mom at the Ford dealership where we would follow her to the house. I stopped and picked up a long stem rose on the way. When I went into the Ford dealership to get Sadie's mom, I saw pictures of the great Henry Ford on the wall. After studying Napoleon Hill's books over the years, I had developed a profound respect for the man who had dreamed that everyone could own an automobile and had covered the earth with his dream. His dream is still very much alive today.

As we drew near to Sadie's home in Derby, Kansas, just on the outskirts of Wichita, I gazed out the window at the many different crops on the farmlands. I thought about my subconscious and how I had created this whole story in my mind. I'd visualized the upcoming moment thousands of times over the years. I looked at the crops and thought about what Napoleon said about the subconscious mind being likened to a "fertile garden where weeds will grow in abundance if seeds of desirable crops aren't sown therein." I had unlocked the key to my subconscious and was aware of what I did. I had followed the instructions in an old book (to the letter), and I was now seeing its whole philosophy unfold right before my eyes!

What had seemed like an eternity of separation now made it feel like just yesterday Sadie had been born. So much had happened over the course of the past thirteen years. On this drive, I couldn't say much. I was very silent, and like I was watching a movie on fast forward, I realized more than ever that we have the canvas in our minds to paint the picture of our lives with our thoughts.

When we finally arrived, I hid around the corner, one house away. Sadie lived across the street from a cemetery, so I stopped for a second and prayed for the dead spirits. With a giant swallow and now finding it hard to breathe, I took the first few steps toward the dream I had conceived in my mind many years ago. Khalil, being a perfectionist, got on the ground to get the right angle. Then he ran across the lawn for better positioning. Not only was I going to have this moment in my heart forever, but I was also going to have it on film forever.

I then gained speed and went toward the door with the biggest smile of my life—now my return to happiness was seeing my daughter again! When I knocked and the door opened, Sadie looked like she had just seen a real life superhero! This was the moment I had dreamt about for so many years. The "impossible" had become fully realized. And in that moment, the love I felt as our hearts came together is a feeling I hope everyone can feel at some time in life.

For years, Sadie had been asking me, "Dad, why can't you come and visit me at my home?" I had never explained the reason to her, but the more she had asked, the harder I had practiced visualization and writing about my sincere desire to see her and be free. That afternoon, I finally told my daughter why I hadn't been allowed in the U.S. for so long. I looked her in the eyes and spoke from the heart, the only way I knew how to speak now. I held her hands and told her about the mistake that had cost me our spending more time together, and I told her how sorry I was that I hadn't always been there when she needed me the most. She was very accepting of my truth. I teared up pretty heavily, but Sadie squeezed my hand and said three words with more emotion than I had ever heard come from her mouth: "It's okay, Dad."

Hearing those words made me feel like King Kong had just jumped off my back. I was so enthusiastic that I didn't know what to do with myself. So the next logical thing to do was go shopping and get Sadie whatever her heart most desired. It was a time to celebrate. I know that this whole experience made her feel awkward at first. God knows that if my dad had been away from my hometown and showed up unannounced after twelve years, I would have been in a state of shock as well. But seeing the look in her eyes made me know that Sadie was going to be a big part of my return to happiness for eternity. It's amazing what a bond we parents can have with our kids. When we look them in the eyes, we can see ourselves in so many ways. The gift I was given on that day still seems like a dream, and I will hold it in my heart for all eternity.

We spent some time together. We went to a Wichita Thunder hockey game. I used to play for the team, and when I ran into the general manager, Joel Lomurno, he gave me free tickets in the perfect spot, right on the center ice line, for which I was very grateful. At the game, I caught a Frisbee out of the air and gave it to Sadie. I nearly went head over heels into the seats in front of me while snatching it, but Sadie just laughed her face off and was proud that her dad had caught a Frisbee for her. I was in Wichita for four days. I stayed one night at a hotel and the other nights at Sadie's grandmother's place because she was away on vacation. Khalil and I would walk down to the Sonic fast-food chain about a mile down the road and eat chili dogs and cheesy fries—talk about gourmet. We always just looked at each other in amazement, saying, "Look where we are now!"

My major dream had come true through filming the movie—I had gotten my one wish granted—to see my daughter. But now what? What was I going to do with my newfound freedom and the project I had worked so passionately on for the past few years? It was time to see what happened next!

PART II: DIVIDENDS

CHAPTER 1
A FORTUITOUS FLIGHT

Khalil had to go to Montreal for a week to put on a show, so I decided to visit the City of Angels to try and rekindle an old friendship and get into the mode to cut up our film. I felt Los Angeles was the place to be if we wanted to get exposure. For me, the film was about spreading the global message of happiness, but L.A., as much as I love it, is very far from Southeast Asia. The values there are somewhat different, although you would have to visit both places fully to understand that difference. Hollywood has made and broken a lot of people over the years, and living proof was evident everywhere.

My flight from Wichita to Los Angeles meant changing flights in Denver. In the Denver airport, I was so busy jamming to my tunes on my iPod that I didn't hear that there were two flights to L.A. and my gate had been changed. Eventually, I was starting to wonder why we hadn't boarded yet. Then I heard the boarding call. It wasn't until I had gotten on the wrong plane and someone told me

I was in the wrong seat that I realized my mistake. I ran up to the crew, begging them to let me stay on this flight. To my blessing, there was one seat left...beside a man named Greg Rhodes. When I sat down next to Greg, I was sweating and my palms were soaked, but Greg was perfectly calm. He had this Zen-like aura about him, and I was instantly calm in his presence. As the plane took off for L.A., Greg and I became acquainted.

Greg told me he was an actor. Then he saw that I had my copy of Napoleon Hill's book in my hands. Everywhere I take that book, I get onlookers either asking me, "What book is that?" or "Where do I get a copy?" I get excited telling them about all the gifts inside the book that can really help them overcome insecurities and reach whatever goals they want to attain. So Greg started sharing some of his ideas and beliefs with me, and big surprise, I found out that Greg, like me, had also been born in July. Finding another sensitive Cancer in my path had become the norm for me. Greg told me about his friend, who had been involved in the production of a film about happiness that featured spiritual giants like Rev. Michael Beckwith and Jack Canfield.

It was so cool that Greg and I had so much in common. When we flew into the worst turbulence I had experienced in years and he saw the worried look on my face, Greg laughed and said, "Don't worry, Ryan; you're in safe hands. Even if we crash, there is no death; death is just a transition. You can't kill energy!" I believed that our spirits are eternal. But I really was looking forward to living a physical experience for a while in California. Greg spoke of Agape Spiritual Center, founded by Rev. Michael Beckwith, whose name I knew from *The Secret* and the book *Spiritual Liberation.* He recommended strongly that I go visit the Center, which I hoped to do, but at this point, number one on my list was being grounded in my purpose.

I couldn't wait to have a tangible product of what Khalil

and I had experienced in Southeast Asia. The start of the film would have a brief summary of my past. I could have gone on forever in the film about what I could have/should have done differently, but now I knew it had all been for a reason. Even on this day when I had missed my plane, it had happened for a reason because now I was talking to Greg. And little did I know then that Greg's friend not only would become a serious ally and believer in *Return to Happiness*, but he was going to give me some insights about the business behind making a film on happiness.

CHAPTER 2
IN LA LA LAND

"Isn't it funny," I thought to myself, "how for years I wanted to live in Los Angeles?" I had dreamed of Disneyland as a kid and my mom and dad had taken me there a few times. I was hooked on California. I loved the Beach Boys, the movies, skateboarding, surfing—anything that was California. When I heard Katy Perry sing her California song, I dreamed of being there. And on my gratitude list for the past many years, I had always said I was grateful to be living in California, knowing it would happen if I just believed and acted as if it already had. I knew it; I could feel it; living there would be just a matter of time. In my younger days, I would party in West Hollywood at the Viper Room and the Garden of Eden, hit after-hours clubs, and run wild, thinking I was some sort of big shot. Now I was moving to the City of Angels to edit a film.

When I arrived at the airport, an old friend picked me up whom I hadn't seen in four years. Like me, he had undergone some serious adversities in his life and was in the process of making amends. He had been married, divorced, and was now clean and sober. He had been afraid for his life in Vancouver, so he had moved to L.A. where he now ran a treatment center and helicopter business, doing tours all over the massive city. As different as we both were, we shared a lot of the same attributes. We hugged and couldn't stop talking for hours about where our paths had led us. God, I had seen him nearly die a few times because of his reckless use of crack and the narcotic sedative GHB. Through everything, I had always cared for him, and I knew the feeling was mutual.

He let me crash at his place in Malibu, and he brought me along with him to show me his work helping others recovering from addiction. I felt good being of service to people yet again. I also found a place to stay since Khalil would be joining me in a week. I was getting fairly attached to Malibu, but the rent there was a little out of my league.

I found a nice apartment on the main drag in Santa Monica, on the corner of Bicknell and Main, and rented it for three months. We had no car, and I had no driver's license, but being close to the beach was a huge bonus. If I'm not close to the mountains and the water, I feel out of alignment with my inner being. Just the sound of water gives me deep insights and a connection to my higher self. In fact, I can actually feel water and the power of Mother Nature talking to me. The apartment had a gym and a great restaurant, M Street Kitchen, was below the apartment with top-notch food and service.

As soon as Khalil arrived, we got down into editing mode. It was my job to write the voiceover to the best of my ability and tell the story through my eyes. Khalil's job was to match the story with all the shots we had taken on the adventure. We made due with a wireless microphone from the Sony XD camera so we could do dummy voiceovers to see how the pictures on the screen would match the story I was telling.

The trip was so fresh in our minds and hearts that, initially, we thought the editing process would be easy. I guess we overestimated the job we had made for ourselves. It wasn't as if we had an immediate deadline. But I had it firmly in my mind that I wanted the premiere to be sometime in the summer. I also didn't let the dream of getting distribution out of my mind for a second.

Something happened to Khalil and me in California. I love the state so much, but we had just been exposed to so much in the past few months that we had no idea how much it had affected us on all levels. We would walk to the promenade, one of the biggest outdoor malls in the U.S. It was so crowded and focused on materialism. Khalil and I had our laid back Asian clothes on, and we would just shake our heads, wishing we were back in Laos where we could eat like kings for ten dollars a day. Khalil especially felt out of his element since he had never been to Southern California before.

I was also still reeling from the most emotional reunion of my life. If I'd had my wish—with all due respect to her mom—Sadie would have been with me now. It's amazing what effects the people we love can have on us. I was feeling very lost in California. I wasn't the life of the party anymore. My path in life was lit up in lights before me, but to follow that path, we had to get through the film-editing process, which was somewhat tedious and very time-consuming. Rather than go to nightclubs and fine restaurants, we stayed focused. We ate off plastic plates in our condo—not that we were living in poverty, but the cost of where we were living was enough to live on for five years in Cambodia. The dirt roads of the bike ride seemed very distant from the busy streets of L.A. where high-end cars were the norm. I had found it just as pleasing to ride a bike through the countryside of Southeast Asia, letting the humidity rush through my veins, as I ever had living the highlife. In Southeast Asia, I had felt so free that city life now took some getting used to again. I can go one step further—Southeast Asia had become my second home.

Khalil and I had spent so much time together over the past three months that living together wasn't as easy as in the beginning stages. We missed the days of adventure where we wouldn't know what the day held. Now, persistence, drive, and focus were needed to make our dream into a physical reality. Khalil had also just broken up with his sweetheart, so I knew he was lonely. We shared a lot of tears in L.A. But we also had some moments of frustration with each other. He loved to sleep in, while I always wanted to get an early start to my workday. I was not one to wait around for an opportunity. My motto was "Let's get 'er done," and I felt there was no time like the present to move into action. I went out and purchased a whiteboard where I wrote down daily, weekly, and monthly goals for what I wanted done. The last thing I wanted was to treat Khalil like an employee—I saw our relationship as more of a partnership—but I also felt I had to keep us moving forward.

Late starts became our norm, but once Khalil was up and at it, with coffee in hand and the best muffin known to man from M Street Kitchen, he was on top of his game. Then the computer would get in the way. The hard drive we had was pretty small for all the footage we had captured. And the computer had a mind of its own—it wouldn't stop stalling and having glitches! Sometimes, I thought I would have to take Khalil to an insane asylum as he would yell at the top of his lungs, "#%@#*! computer!" We did a lot of pacing in that apartment; I'm surprised the carpets didn't wear out. Some days were so long and frustrating that I think a lot of people would have given up if they had been in our place. But we just kept saying to each other, "Persistence will make winners out of us, and if we are to teach people through this film never to give up, then we can't give up now." And as we worked and our vision became clearer, the film kept changing in good ways toward becoming the final product we wanted to bring to fruition.

We only had a few nights on the town and they would always end early. We didn't talk to many people because we were so focused on our work and it was hard to discuss our challenges with other people. We wanted to keep the story of *Return to Happiness* to ourselves for now because we didn't really know what the final product would entail.

During this time, Serinda invited us to an event she was putting on in Hollywood at the Bagatelle restaurant. I think that was the first time I realized we were in showbiz land. At the event, I saw the actress Brooke Burke and her family. I met Quddus, the host of ABC's *Duets*, and I met the cast of *Breakout Kings*. It was funny seeing Serinda at her event—she was very well-spoken and in an evening gown, a real contrast to her dirty bike shorts and a sunburn. As I looked around the room, I wondered how many of these people had been where Khalil and I now were? When I tried talking to a few people about the bike-riding experience, they looked at me like I was half-nuts, but I felt grateful to Serinda for opening my eyes to the cause. That night, an episode of *Master Chef* was being filmed at the restaurant. When our food came, it looked a tad different than the food we had eaten in Southeast Asia. Khalil and I looked at each other and chuckled at where we had been compared to where we were now.

That night as we headed home early, Khalil and I felt more educated about Hollywood. I don't think people at the event had really known how to take me. In Hollywood, it's all about who you know, what show you are on, and who knows you. But I had treated everyone the same that night, always with a smile. If I have one powerful message that will make a profound impact on a person's life, it's "Just be you."

At the end of May, we were approaching the two-month mark of working on the editing, and I would say we were 70 percent done. I had just finished doing a voiceover, and for some reason, I was nervous. I wanted it to be perfect, and it was my first time in a studio. My usual confidence in front of the camera didn't shine through me in the soundproof studio because I was so intent on perfecting the masterpiece we'd worked so hard on. When Khalil added the voiceover to the film, I was very dissatisfied with the product, so I made a decision! I woke up one morning and said, "I think we should go to New York City."

I had been in contact with a friend there who had also been involved with the Somaly Mam Foundation. Through Skype, we'd had many wonderful talks about life and she had educated me on the issues of human trafficking and sex slavery. She had known about my efforts to make the film and been very supportive and was willing to do what she could to help me finish the film in New York and begin to promote it.

Khalil had also begun talking to a girl in Montreal, so I said, "Here's the dealio. You fly to Montreal and spend a week with your girl. (His U.S. visa was only for two months anyway while I had been blessed to get six.) I'll fly to New York City." We decided Khalil could finish the majority of the work in Montreal, and then come to New York so we could put the finishing touches on it. There were studios in New York, and I knew Khalil and I needed some time apart to breathe.

My friend found me an apartment on the upper east side of Manhattan while Khalil returned to Montreal. Those few weeks apart would open up the channels of our creative imagination and allow us to ingest everything we had seen and experienced in the last five months. Because of the computer problems, we had also lost half of the film we had edited, so we needed a break from our frustrations. The old Ryan would have been angry about this situation, but I knew it had happened for a reason. We were both anxious to finish, but we were also perfectionists who had to keep tweaking the film until it was right. The music had to match the emotion that was caught on film in the moment. We wanted to hook the viewer's attention to the full magnitude of our message. We would keep working on it until we were both satisfied and had achieved our goal.

CHAPTER 3
NEW YORK CITY—THE CENTER OF THE WORLD

I needed a change of scenery and thought New York was the perfect place. I had never visited the Big Apple before, but now I would witness its size and scope. Not only were there sound studios there, but I thought I could help the Somaly Mam organization located there. When my friend Izzy from the organization picked me up at the airport, she said "Welcome to New York!" We jumped into a cab, and a few minutes after leaving JFK Airport, I saw the gigantic skyscrapers and bright lights and was blown away.

The first few days were surreal. Izzy was a champion tour guide, although she made me figure out the giant subway system on my own. We went down to Times Square, and everywhere I saw the major influence that the Rockefellers, Carnegies, and Donald Trump had in building New York into a powerful city of wealth. I couldn't believe how many people lived in this city, and I was engrossed by its history. I now knew why New Yorkers are so proud. The city rarely sleeps.

While I did a lot of sightseeing in New York, I also had to get back to work. I still needed to do a new voiceover for the documentary. I also was starting to feel a sense of displacement about where I was supposed to be. I did not feel safe in Vancouver any longer. I had not felt that I fit into L.A., and now in New York, I also found myself feeling uncomfortable. What was supposed to be exciting and adventurous became nothing of the sort. I secluded myself in my small apartment on the upper east side of Manhattan, at times pacing and wondering where I had gone wrong. I felt disconnected from my spirit although the people I knew there had my back and were well-intentioned toward me. Old habits that had provided me a daily reprieve from stress, such as weight training and running, became hard for me. I found myself sleeping in, depressed with no sense of purpose or direction. I was a lost soul in a big city, and I missed my family tremendously. I tried to write, but the creative faculties of my mind were blocked by negative thoughts of "Why am I here?" even though I was in an amazing city.

When Khalil thought he had the film almost finished, he hopped a bus to New York. We still needed to redo the voiceover, so I had found a really nice man named Duane in the Tribeca area of New York who owned a small studio. Duane really loved the project, and that meant a lot to me because he'd worked with some famous people in the business. It was a rainy night when we found ourselves in Duane's studio. This time, I gave it my all, feeling more relaxed than before. I knew I had to get it done that night because Khalil had to catch his bus home. We got it done, but I still wasn't fully satisfied. I felt a lot of anxiety because the project wasn't forming into the vision I saw in my mind. But I had faith that Khalil would match the voiceover to the film and music. It only took him a few days to complete it all, and then he FedExed the "finished" product to the

Somaly Mam organization for me to pick up. I opened the package with excitement. A few ladies who worked at the organization were also excited, wanting to see the footage of Somaly and the girls. They knew I wanted the film to raise awareness for the organization, to be a voice for it as much as possible.

We popped the DVD into one of the office computers and began the first viewing of *Return to Happiness*. My heart sank after the first ten minutes. It was missing something! I always watch other people's faces when they are viewing something I've created, and if there's no emotional reaction, then I haven't done my job right. We wanted the viewer to feel like he was present with me as he watched the film, but that connection was not being made. As I watched it, I rated the film as only a seven out of ten, but after we ejected the DVD, I said it was a six, tops. I was probably overly hard on myself, but I wanted the film to be something people would not only relate to, but remember for a long time after watching it.

In my mind, it was missing two very important ingredients: interviews between the different segments and quotes describing each segment's purpose. The quotes had to open the viewer's mind. They had to connect the viewer to what he was about to watch and make it clear why he was watching it in the first place. And without interviews of me and others explaining our purposes, then the viewer was only watching me in action in Southeast Asia, without being clear on my purpose.

The ladies at the Somaly Mam organization tried to reassure me, saying, "This is only the beginning." But I didn't have much to say. I left the office with my tail between my legs. The job was still a long ways from being done.

I know now that I was searching for answers from within. Sadie and my parents were going to visit me for ten days in July, so I was counting every second until their arrival. I realized the one thing I was lacking the most was love. I'm the type of person who is driven by emotion, so when I come to a decision, it usually comes fast and there's not a whole lot anyone can say to make me change it once I make up my mind. Now I heard an inner voice telling me, "Cancel your family trip to New York and go back to Vancouver; you need to spend time with your daughter in the tranquility of nature." So that was that; I booked a flight the next day back to Canada. If I saw the two people back home who wanted to harm me, I would just call the police.

I was in fear of my family's safety, but I also knew I was no longer involved in their business and I wasn't who they thought I was. I had to think deeply about the fear I felt over this issue. My mind was strong! I had made it this far. And I knew that the universe had a plan for me. Even though these people might still have it out for me, how could I let their negative energy influence my experience? God knew I had made the film *Return to Happiness* for everyone on the planet. If I could walk away from a dangerous lifestyle, then why couldn't others find a way as well? How could I let evil into my very core essence of love, compassion, and understanding? My daughter needed me, and as much fun as showing her the Big Apple might have been, I felt most connected to my source when I could take her for a walk in the mountains. That's where I could talk freely to Sadie about this life we live and explain that it's not all rainbows all the time. I kissed New York goodbye and flew out the next morning with my heart full of gratitude for what I had learned there.

CHAPTER 4
VANCOUVER—THE LAST LEG OF COMPLETION

Sadie and my parents welcomed me at the Vancouver airport with open arms! I couldn't believe how Sadie had grown in the three months since I had last seen her. She jumped on me and yelled, "Daddio!" I was in the presence of family. Although grateful for my time in California and New York, family love is what I needed the most. I was emotionally exhausted. And I knew what had to be done next! First was showing my daughter the best three weeks known to man or woman. Second, I needed to hire a cameraman to shoot some interviews for the film. Third, I had to book Khalil a flight to Vancouver for a couple of days after Sadie left so we could tighten the film up to perfection. I decided to call my friend Mark Hemstock, with whom I had done some work in the past over in Europe, to film the interviews. He was elated to hear my voice since we hadn't talked in some time, and I thought it only fitting to ask for his help since he had been part of *Return to*

Happiness' inception about a year earlier.

I had Mark come over to my parents' house so we could film the interviews in a nice setting in front of the fire. During the interviews, I had no plan but simply spoke from the heart—the only way I knew how—about the different experiences along my journey. Sadie's energy helped me in those interviews. She was such a driving force for the film. I was proud to see how much she had grown while we were both on our separate paths. But a father and daughter's bond is unbreakable and eternal. No matter how old Sadie gets, she will always know that I have her back, no matter what. And to look into her eyes and see my own looking back is an indescribable blessing for me.

I took her zip trekking at Whistler Mountain. It felt epic to be in nature, flying through the forest at high speeds, upside down at times, looking down at canyons full of glacier water. Thank God for that day's memories. We walked around the village after the tour, but our energy was so amped up that we went for a long hike on one of the nature trails to soak up some shade. We also got in some awesome golf games. I was getting to know my daughter more and she was getting to know me. We must have played golf fifteen of the twenty days I spent with her. We shared our birthdays together and bonded like never before.

Goodbyes are only easy if the person isn't going to be gone a long time! The whole Sadie-Dad thing gets harder for me every time. We said our goodbyes, and as usual, I was like butter, yet had to be strong.

I only had two weeks to finish the film before the premiere screening and charity event at the University of Miami. My dad flew home with Sadie while Khalil came to finish *Return to Happiness*. We had a deadline, but two weeks was plenty of time to put the final touches on the film. I rewrote the majority of the voiceover and was able to do it with more feeling after watching the footage and reliving the experiences from start to finish. Khalil was really happy with the short interviews exemplifying my perspective on each portion of the film. I'd just had to go into that emotional center deep inside my soul, relive it in my memory bank, and let it flow onto film.

No time was wasted on getting things done, and both Khalil and I were really happy that the computer timeline was working well without any setbacks. So on that first day, we definitely got ahead of ourselves, saying, "This will be done in only a few short days!" The divine had other ideas. Day two, the computer started jamming and we were reliving the L.A. experience all over again. It was a nightmare. Right when we thought we had everything pieced together, Khalil started losing parts of the timeline and had to start rebuilding the project. Thank God for my parents because all I could do was watch and try to be patient while Khalil tried with all his might to keep the cussing to a minimum when things did not come together the way we intended. It all happened for a reason, however. Whenever we would lose something on the film's timeline, we would come up with a better idea of what to insert.

I always say that the more frustrated people get, the more frustration and anxiety they bring into the moment. My mom was a "rock." She saw how badly we wanted to finish this project in a positive manner and move on so the world could see our journey. It's tough at times not to run your body and mind down when you get so emotionally involved in a project you care about so much. Every time Khalil would start pulling at his hair and feel disconnected, my mom and I would just hug him with compassion and full faith that everything would be done in just the right way God intended. More than ever, I could hear Helen's voice saying, "You guys are in each other's life for a reason." So when things weren't working, I would take Khalil for walks through the forest and we would just talk about life.

Nothing in life that you create comes easily all the time. God, or that Higher Power, puts obstacles in our lives to test our spiritual faculties so we can learn what we are made of. If this project was supposed to be easy, we would have had it done in California. It was meant for us to finish it in Vancouver where my loving parents could share their wisdom about dealing with adversity and pushing on toward your dreams!

Day in and day out, we would spend hours upon hours giving all our energy to completing *Return to Happiness*. The Miami premiere we had scheduled was now only a week away. When people asked me, "Will it be done in time?" with all my faith and determination, I would reply, "Yes, of course it will. It will be done in a special and unique way that will have an emotional impact for the viewer." I saw now why it hadn't been finished in L.A. or New York City. The little things had to be great so it could have the most profound effect possible on its audience.

I called my old friend Jim Conrad, a local radio personality who had contacts with studios that did voiceover productions. When Jim called in a favor to a local studio, I was able to get the job done free of charge. I had one shot left now since the next day I would board a flight to Miami. The film was done, the quotes I desired were inserted—my voice explaining the journey was the only missing ingredient. I meditated on what I needed to do. I tried to relax my body as much as possible to get into a good feeling place before I spoke *Return to Happiness'* story into a microphone.

Jim, a true pro, coached me through the process. Thank God that at this point in my life, I felt coachable. That's a trait many of us should incorporate—be coachable! Even the greats will tell you that being open to being coached is what makes one a master. My energy was so high that I tended to talk without breathing at times. I was so excited and nervous because I had to nail it. I wanted to stand at the microphone instead of sitting. I felt I could feed more of my emotion while standing. So I got comfortable and started to speak into the mic from my heart. Jim had to stop me a few times to remind me to pause more between words. I knew by the look in Khalil's eyes that it was flowing just the way we had both imagined. I closed my eyes on many parts of the script, which I had mostly memorized. With eyes closed, I could see myself in the environment I spoke about. I could feel myself at the AFESIP center in Cambodia. I relived the entire experience in my mind as the words rolled off my tongue. And with comparative ease compared to L.A. and New York City, it all sounded right. All that was left now was to match the voice to the film and then put it on DVD to view.

I graciously thanked Jim and the studio for their help. The voice was added to the film and in the morning I would have it imported onto a DVD. We were done as far as we knew, but we would have one last surprising hurdle. When we got back to my parents' house, Khalil, Mom, Dad, and I had a group hug together. The film was finally done for the world to see! And we were ready to watch it complete and in its entirety. So Khalil pressed play….

The music started off just perfectly and we both smiled at each other, I looked back at my mom and she looked at me with her proud eyes. Then, just like a dagger to the throat, I saw *Return to Happines.... Happiness* was spelled wrong! I had to hold Khalil back from screaming at the top of his lungs. I did my best not to get upset and said, "It's only a test! Let's make the change and wait patiently for it to get fixed." Khalil only had four hours before he had to fly home, so we were cutting it close. But when you just accept that everything happens for a reason, things fall off your back like water. We found another spelling mistake on the Somaly Mam quote and corrected it as well. In a few hours, the film would be done. Miami would be a huge success, no matter what.

The film was done after just a few hours of waiting patiently. This segment of my and Khalil's paths had come to an end for now. Khalil was dropped off at the airport and had a smooth ride to Montreal. I knew he wanted to get on with his life; he needed some much deserved head space after all we had been through. We had shared so many emotions together with so many people, and it had all started as a dream conceived in Montreal back in December, 2011. We wondered what people would think of our film, but at this point, I was going to savor our victory in completing *Return to Happiness.* We had proven to ourselves something we had known from the start—that desire, mixed with persistence and faith, would give us something that nobody could ever take away from us. Our experience was life-changing. We would never be the same. We had touched other people's lives in the creation process, and they had returned the favor. What was once a vision was now tangible. We had found the root of happiness within ourselves by learning that if you do what you love, that is where you will find your bliss. Now I could go to Miami holding my head high! The greatest lesson I learned in completing the film was how important is one's willpower! It was the key ingredient, mixed with our strong desire and faith, that led to our finished product. No other way than through our willpower could this film have been finished. I can wholeheartedly say that this experience put every other obstacle I had ever had to surmount in my life into perspective. My so called failures and tests in life became crystal clear. The only time I had ever failed to achieve something that I had truly desired was when I had failed to use my willpower to back up my burning desire and unwavering faith just to "get it done!" I learned that just showing up, being present, and having tireless work ethic are the main ingredients for any kind of success in life. I'd needed to come to enlightenment in order to realize a dream; it may sound harsh, but sometimes you have to be willing to die for the truth. And when you are, and you refuse to give up, the universe has a way of getting behind you and pushing you forward, regardless of what anyone else says or thinks.

CHAPTER 5
THE MIAMI PREMIERE AND A FILM FESTIVAL

It was humid and windy when I landed in Miami. A tropical storm was on the horizon. I checked into my hotel, wishing Khalil were with me because I always like to celebrate accomplishments with the people who have been with me every step of the way. When I got to the hotel, I was able to catch up with Izzy from foundation, and I was treated like royalty by the event sponsors. These people really cared with all their hearts about the girls in Cambodia.

And then, there I was in a theatre, seeing the journey that not only I, but my family and friends, desired for me so badly to finish. It felt wonderful to have so much support from such great people. I'll never forget that day. It might not have been exactly as I had imagined, but it was special because the people who had made it happen did so with caring hearts. We only had sixty people in the theatre, but we raised some money for the Somaly Mam Foundation, and every little bit helped. The couple hosting the event had promised that the theatre would be full, but a lot of people who had committed ended up not coming. Unfortunately, the word had spread in Miami that the film was only about sex trafficking. People didn't know that *Return to Happiness* was much more than that. The film had many teaching aspects that could be applied by people anywhere in the world to give them more fulfilling lives.

The people who did come were very inspired by the film, and that's what counted. I had begun the film thinking if it could help just one person, I would have done my job. This film wasn't driven by money. I was proud that the finished product looked very professional, but I was most moved when I saw that there wasn't a dry eye in the house when the movie was over. The parts in Cambodia at the AFESIP center were enough to get the coldest person in the world to swallow his tongue. Now I felt that all of my and Khalil's hard work, the early mornings in Asia, all the smiles and tears—they had all been worth it.

After the Miami premiere, I flew to Montrose, Colorado to meet an old friend I hadn't seen in twelve years—Ray Cody. Let me tell you, Ray is one of the most authentic, loving men I have ever met. For many years, he has practiced the art of determining his own destiny through creative thought. I had first met Ray when I was twenty and playing in the Central Hockey League, where he was a referee. Although I was a wild one, Ray had seen something in me. Maybe a younger version of himself? Whatever the case, Ray taught me how certain principles can reap astonishing rewards of peace of mind and financial security.

The summer of '99 when Sadie was born, Ray was by my side as a mentor. He taught me through his actions; in fact, the way he lived with such generosity and grace made me envious at times. Ray was a successful, self-made millionaire, but he would never tell you that. He was humble and very hardworking. But most of all, he loved to help others. At a time when my mind wasn't ready to understand the whole manifestation and self-creation process, Ray demonstrated certain attributes that I would later understand. He owned a number of companies and an apartment complex that he managed to perfection through organization and passion. Whatever he did, he did with confidence and full faith that he would attract success with ease. His life meant something to him and everyone who came across his path. He treated everyone with compassion. At the time, he was taking care of an elderly lady who did not have much time left. Ray gave her a room at his complex, free of charge, and he took care of her like she was his mom. He even changed her diapers. As I watched him care for her, I couldn't fully grasp the significance of his heartfelt desire to make this lady's last days special. Ray loved and cared for her. He also was involved with youth programs and inspiring others to be great. He was never too busy to help anyone he could, and on top of it all, he had an awesome sense of humor.

Ray gave, and in return, he was always rewarded with amazing opportunities because he was just that kind of person. Who wouldn't want to do business with someone who had such love for his fellow man? Ray told me that he wanted to leave this world a better place. He wanted to create a legacy and be a role model for his daughter and the community. He knew I was very lost at the time, but he never judged me. He tried to explain to me how the prefrontal cortex of the brain was like a computer switchboard. I didn't give much thought to his teachings at the time, but he had this way of making me have hope. A true friend, he was there the night Sadie was born.

Ray and I reconnected in 2010 when he sent me a friend request on Facebook which I instantly accepted. I saw by his Facebook photos that he had continued to reap abundance in his life. He was now married to a lovely lady and had moved to the magical ski town of Telluride, Colorado. He had gone into business with Jack Nicklaus, one of golf's all-time greats, on a high-end bed and breakfast that was featured in *Forbes* magazine. On Facebook, I saw pictures of Ray's family, Ray playing Santa for kids, and his involvement as a huge pillar of strength in his community. I had to see Ray and the universe was lining it all up for me. Ray picked me up in his plane in Montrose to fly us over the beautiful Rocky Mountains into the town of Telluride. It was amazing to see Ray again and to hear about his family and business life. When I asked him what he attributed his success to, he said he built his family relations and business life on the principles of two books—Robert Kiyosaki's *Rich Dad, Poor Dad* and Napoleon Hill's *Think and Grow Rich*. He told me that everything he had in his life was due to the intangible spiritual principles he practiced on a daily basis.

Ray's work ethic and pleasing personality set into motion a newly conceived property management company that became number one in Telluride. His accounts were marvelous because of the service he provided to others. He served others with such integrity that he attracted other big accounts to his company. He had financial freedom and, of course, faith because he lived by the divine laws of nature. He had always aimed high, and let me tell you, he was only just getting started. In Telluride, he manages Tom Cruise's home, and he takes care of it with the same pride he would his own home or any other. He moved across the street from Telluride's biggest developer, Steve Finger, and they have now formed an alliance, building many hotels in the United States with a producer of the *Men in Black* movie series. Ray is living proof that when you aim high, work hard, and have faith, there's nothing that will stand in the way of your attracting the highest levels of success. Ray seemed to live his life without fear. He always dove right in with action, and he was never too big to go the extra mile to help his staff in their labor.

It just so happened that Telluride was hosting a film

festival the week I was there. I'd had no idea about it—and it was one of the world's top five film festivals. When I had met with Helen before leaving for Southeast Asia, she had told me she saw me at a film festival in the United States. I had tearfully told her that I wasn't allowed in the country any longer. Now I knew without a doubt that when you tap into the power of the human mind with focus and desire, the intangible forces of the universe will bend nature to make happen whatever you focus on! Everything that had happened was now almost more than I could believe, but it had only happened because I had believed. Here I was at this wonderful man's home in Telluride, Colorado during a film festival—perhaps the very one Helen had foreseen.

Soon I met a gentleman who had a lot of influence in the festival. He said it was too bad that I wasn't able to get my film in on time and they couldn't break the rules for me, but he made a call to the local television station to arrange for *Return to Happiness* to be broadcast. I was proud that the film was given praise and thought to be a worthy creation that people would enjoy. That made my heart sing.

One of my old idols, Bill Murray, was in town for the festival. As a kid, Mr. Murray had made me laugh my tail off, and even now when I watch the timeless movie *Caddyshack*, I find it hard to contain myself. In high school, I had memorized every word of the film, and I used to recite it to my friends. Now, everywhere I went in Telluride, Bill Murray's name was mentioned, and from what I was told, thousands of people had swarmed him with autograph and photo requests.

Knowing Bill Murray was in Telluride was cool, but there was no way I was going to be in a big crowd swarming him. Instead, I made it definite in my mind that I would meet him. I found out he was staying kitty corner to Ray's bed and breakfast, so I thought I would write up a nice letter, telling Mr. Murray how much respect I had for him as an actor and asking him whether he could watch the film I had produced. My plan was to give the letter to the concierge at the hotel where he was staying, and hopefully, the letter would find its way into his hands and he would get back to me. Just moments after sealing the letter in an envelope, I went into a room and lay on the ground, envisioning myself meeting Mr. Murray one on one! I felt it, I played the scene in my mind for at least half an hour, and I got so emotionally involved with the feeling that I believed the meeting would actually happen. I'd done it before. I knew I had the tools, the thought-energy in the creative faculties of my mind to make it happen. "It's a done deal," I said to myself. Then, I proceeded across the street to give the movie to the concierge.

At that moment, a white Escalade pulled up thirty feet from the hotel when no one else was in sight. I intuitively knew who was in it. Yes, Mr. Murray stepped out and we locked eyes immediately. Jokingly, I said, "Hey, it's Frank, right?" He replied, "That's one of the names they call me." We both had a laugh. And then, there I was having a face-to-face discussion with Bill Murray. It was really cool because he was very open and friendly. I've never been the type to get star-struck since I believe all people are made from the same stuff. But his comedic ways had always had me, my family, and friends in stitches. I told him, "I had no idea there was a film festival here this week! I'm from Canada and I just finished producing this film and I think you would like it; it's very heartfelt." He looked at me seriously for a moment and saw I was not trying to hassle him for an autograph or picture. So we talked for a while on the nature of what my film was about. And then he said he was very much looking forward to watching it. We shook hands and gave each other hugs. I could feel his energy and had such a tough time keeping a straight face while talking to him.

As Bill Murray started to walk off, I told him my dad would kill me if I didn't take a picture with him because my dad was such a fan of his. He said, "Well, we don't need your dad killing you, Ryan. We need you around for a while." So we put our arms around each other, Bill holding the movie in his hand, and his wife took a really cool picture. And that was that.

How do we manifest? I've explained many times so far along the journey of this book, and I will say it again. I saw the event like it had happened already! There was no doubt. So the more "coincidences" like this one that happen in my life, the more firmly I believe that anyone open to visualization, belief, and faith can do the exact same thing. Sometimes, the procedure works faster than at other times. The key is to feel with certainty that the event has taken place, and to let the energy flow throughout one's entire body. If I'm not relaxed and in a somewhat meditative state, I find it more difficult. Although as more manifestations have taken place for me and fairly rapidly, the more I've come to realize that all we need to do is come into vibrational alignment with our desire.

The funny thing is that earlier that day my new friend Steve Finger was going to take me over to a big hotel development he owned called The Elements to introduce me to Ben Affleck and get a copy of the film into his hands. I had made eye contact with Ben earlier that morning while he was being interviewed on a panel about a film in which he had recently starred. He looked pretty tired, and I'm sure being involved in a festival and having such a recognizable face can be overwhelming at times. When Steve came to take me over to his hotel, I was in my room envisioning my meeting with Bill Murray so he left me alone. We did go over to the Elements a little later, but by then, the Affleck family had already left for home. My focus was on another subject, which is one of the main points I'm trying to convey—when we become mentally and physically focused on too many subjects, it's hard to get your main desire to come into fruition. That's why I always say, "Make the main thing the main thing, most of the time." The main thing has to dominate with so much thought-energy that the intangible forces of the universe will deliver a physical solution to it with intense speed. Others may call it being in the zone, or tuned in, but whatever it's called, this I know: It will work for anyone who lets go of resistant thoughts, and it will draw whatever is desired into his or her experience.

I flew home, really happy about the premiere in Miami and my time in Telluride. I felt things were moving forward for me and the film. Everyone who saw *Return to Happiness* was realizing how insignificant his or her own daily and personal problems really were, and how coming into alignment with a healthier way of living could benefit a person's overall wellbeing. My purpose was being achieved.

CHAPTER 6
AGAPE—UNCONDITIONAL LOVE

A few days after I got back to Vancouver, I received a phone call from a friend at the Somaly Mam Foundation. The actress AnnaLynne McCord was putting on an event in Los Angeles, and just prior to that event would be a gifting event to educate celebrities on the nature of the Somaly Mam Foundation. I had never heard of a gifting event, but since I was invited to attend, I was willing to help in any way I could. Plus, Somaly was going to be there so I would have the opportunity to give her a big hug and get reacquainted.

After few days of downtime in Vancouver, my bags were packed again. When I told my friend in L.A. that I was coming, he agreed to pick me up at the airport, and he arranged for me to meet with staff at Agape Spiritual Center in Culver City, California. I was really excited about this meeting because I knew Rev. Michael Beckwith was the leader of the spiritual center. "The Rev," as he was referred to at Agape, had been featured in the runaway hit *The Secret* and involved in many other books and films. I had seen and studied some of Rev. Beckwith's work, and I knew he had a similar background to myself. Like me, he'd overcome obstacles in his life that had led to an awakening, and ever since, he had used his adversities and wisdom to teach millions of people around the world about unconditional love, compassion, and spiritual wisdom. One thing I do know—Mr. Beckwith is as authentic as they come and his light shines before the world in the flesh and in any TV interviews he does. He's pure truth and lives a life of unconditional love, which is what he stands for. In fact, he named the center Agape because it means "unconditional love" in Greek.

The night before I flew to L.A., my mom and I watched Rev. Beckwith on YouTube. We loved how humble and sincere he was in delivering his message. I really looked up to him for his faith and his ability to inspire others and bring out the best in them. He was the person from *The Secret* whom I wanted to meet the most. Don't get me wrong; I intend to meet Bob Proctor, Lisa Nichols, and Jack Canfield in the near future, and I look up to them with the utmost respect. But there was something about the way the Rev talked about a more harmonious planet built on unconditional love...his soothing voice sounding like gentle music rolling off his tongue. He has touched so many people, and his purpose as a teacher, in my humble opinion, isn't only unique, but fun as well. He makes his services fun, a place to celebrate, and isn't that what life's all about anyway—finding God within you and trying your best to make every day a celebration.

I went to bed that night listening to the Rev speaking. My friend had told me it would be next to impossible for me to meet the Rev, but I didn't believe that for a second. As I lay down in my quiet room and listened to the Rev intently with my eyes closed, I pictured him talking to me. It was just me and the Rev, one-on-one, and he was giving me deep insights into his thoughts about the laws of the universe. He was right in front of me in my imagination, and I didn't take my eyes off him for a second. When I finally became sleepy, I flipped down my laptop and said, "I'm so grateful for meeting you, Rev. Beckwith." Then I fell into a deep sleep in which I dreamt of meeting the Rev; I don't remember exactly how that dream played out, but my subconscious was obviously tapped in from hours of listening to him, visualizing meeting him, and my impressing upon the universe our actual meeting like it had already happened.

In the morning, Mom was up way before me. I could hear her making me oatmeal in the kitchen, and she was going to bring me to the airport. The whole way there, I couldn't stop thinking about what the next few days had in store for me, and meeting the Rev stuck out in bright lights in my mind. Even while clearing customs, listening to music on my iPod, and boarding the plane, I didn't once stop the visualization process. The flight was just over two hours and it went by really quickly. I had a window seat and looked out in amazement at the beautiful landscape of the United States of America. I remembered all the times I'd flown over the States, wishing I could be there, and now I could come and go just like anyone else.

My friend was late picking me up at the airport, but I didn't mind, although it was a hot mid-August day. Finally, after being held up in L.A. traffic, my good friend pulled up, sweaty and apologetic. I told him, "Hey, buddy, what are you going to do? Such is life. We can never force things to happen, and you're here now; that's all that matters." He asked whether I wanted to go drop my gear off where I was staying in West Hollywood, but my mind was on visiting Agape. "Let's go straight to Agape," I replied. "I need to meet the Rev." My friend looked at me like I was nuts and replied, "Brother, I highly doubt he will be there, and on a day like today, he's probably at home or traveling. Getting a meeting with him is close to impossible."

I told my friend, with sheer confidence, "We need to go to the spiritual center right now. I just have a feeling." So he said, "All right, but don't get your hopes up." Right away, we got stuck in gridlock traffic since it was rush hour. My friend got a bit frustrated when we got lost, so we had to ask for directions at a gas station. But not once did I get off my beam of calmness and confidence in my own mind that I would see the Rev that day. My plan was to walk into Agape and ask the staff politely whether I could talk to the Rev, but the universe had other plans....

We finally made it to Culver City and pulled into Agape's almost empty parking lot. My friend drove up to the front of the lot where most of the staff parked. At the exact time we were pulling into the parking spot, a black Lexus pulled in beside us. Lo and behold, it was the Rev! Goosebumps rippled through my body as an intense rush of nonphysical energy radiated from me like a tornado! I calmly got out of the car and looked over at the Rev at the exact moment he looked over at me. "Hello, Mr. Beckwith. How are you today?" I said. The Rev walked over to me and introduced himself, humbly saying, "I'm wonderful. How are you?"

I told him, "I knew I was going to see you today. Actually, I manifested the meeting in my mind over the course of the last day. I'm from Canada, and I really respect everything you live for. I just finished producing a film that is based on many of the principles you teach. It's the Law of Attraction in action. Would you like a copy?" He smiled and said he would love a copy; he explained that he was flying to Atlanta later that day so he would pop it into his laptop and watch it on the way there. We gave each other a big hug and talked for a while about life and both our journeys. My friend told the Rev that we were there to talk to his staff about the possibility of having a premiere for the film at the center. The Rev was so very open and genuine.

It didn't surprise me that he had been given the chance to spread his gifts to the world. When I told him I was also planning to write a book to accompany the film, I asked him whether he would mind if I mentioned how I had manifested our meeting. Laughing, he replied, "Only if you spell my name right," and then he gave me a big hug. He also asked me whether I would be attending the service on Sunday. I told him I wouldn't miss it for the world.

After meeting the Rev, I was introduced to the majority of the staff who welcomed us with open arms. I was told by so many people at the center how the Rev inspires people about the infinite possibilities we all possess. His love is real, and it's powerful because he conveys his message with such sincerity. Agape Spiritual Center was special; it had pure positive energy and I was so happy to be there. I went into the main room where the services are held and saw uplifting pictures of Mother Teresa, Gandhi, the Dali Lama, Nelson Mandela, and several other inspiring people, including a nice picture of the Rev and his wife. A lot of powerful messages had been personified in that room over the years. It's glorious when you can have that feeling of warmth and goodness from positive energy that spreads throughout spaces. I talked in depth about *Return to Happiness*, and I told the staff how honored I would be if they had a screening there. Doris, who was like the Rev's right-hand, had a very magnetic energy about her, and I could tell right away that she had a strong connection to God. She had a great sense of authentic humor as well. She educated me on how the center is run and how busy the Rev is. After thanking her and the staff for their time, my friend and I left. It was important for me to have connected with these people because everything I stood for in life was what they believed in as well.

When we came back for the Sunday service, I learned that Doris had watched the movie. She told me that she couldn't sleep that night, so at 3 a.m., God told her to put the DVD in. Doris took me aside that day and asked me what was my vision for *Return to Happiness*. I told her with the upmost truth, "I see it as a movement, helping others to find peace within themselves and to believe more than anything that happiness is a state of mind that can be cultivated." She obviously liked what I had to say because she introduced me to the Rev's wife, and in no time, I was talking to the Rev again. They were all just real people on a path to giving love and hope to the world, to creating a global community of goodness. How blessed I was to meet like-minded people that day. Thank God that my friend had gotten lost and was late to the airport. The simple reason played out with perfect timing.

This visit to California was short but ever so sweet and gratifying. I had met more people who injected faith and inspiration into my life. This journey was getting wild because the person I had set out to be was a person of such unwavering faith and a spreader of positive aspects, and now, every corner I turned, I was meeting like-minded individuals. I had realized more than ever how energy works, and my life was running like a dream. And it wasn't fancy cars or the fast lane of life that was doing it. It was me meeting wonderful people who had love in their hearts to create a better planet.

On my second day in California, I saw Somaly Mam. She was in the middle of filming some sort of documentary, but when she saw me, she jumped up immediately and gave me a massive embrace. I placed in her hand an opal stone that said "strength," one of her many aspects. She was grateful and held it in her hand during her film interview. She was there for a gala and to promote her cause. I hadn't seen her since Cambodia, although we'd had some Facebook chats. I could see again how she radiated love and with what ease she handles herself, even on a global platform, because she stands for truth and has purpose in her life.

Sina, whom I'd also met in Cambodia, was with Somaly. Now that we were all in L.A., I felt a little out of my element. I'm a nature boy, so what can I say? I love California, but it's a far cry from Vancouver and Cambodia. So bless Somaly for having the courage to spread her cause globally. She's always on the go, whether it's in New York, L.A., Australia, or Singapore. She has a way of touching crowds like I'd never seen before. It's a beautiful thing to see such a being of love stand up for people who are going through what she once did and to back up her words with action.

That same day, I spoke on behalf of the Somaly Mam Foundation at a gifting event at the W Hotel in West Hollywood. I went alone and was told there was a booth set up with bracelets made from the girls in Cambodia and some pamphlets to inform celebrities on the nature of sex slavery and human trafficking. My job was to educate these people by telling them what I had seen in Cambodia and what the foundation's cause was all about. I spoke to many people who made their living in film and television. I recognized some of them, but I'm not an avid TV viewer so I didn't know the majority. I had been told to bring copies of my movie to give to a few people, but I swear, I talked in depth about the cause and Somaly's spirit before I even brought up my movie to anyone. The only reason I wanted to get the movie into a celebrity's hands was because just maybe that person would see how real the epidemic was for the Cambodian people.

I developed some great relationships at the gifting event. I took some pictures with different celebrities, and I smiled proudly from my heart to be there on behalf of Somaly and the girls in Cambodia. One of the event planners, however, felt I was overstepping my boundaries with the celebrities, so without hearing the reason, I was relieved of my duties. It was too bad because I was having a great time and felt I had made some really genuine connections with some of the people there. Still not understanding how being myself was overstepping my boundaries, I went back to my hotel to take a nap before going to the event put on by AnnaLynne McCord.

I was asleep for about two hours when I received a call from one of the ladies in charge of the Somaly Mam Foundation in New York. She was in L.A. and I had just had coffee with her earlier that morning when I had seen Somaly. Now she told me I was uninvited to the event that night because it had gotten back to her that I was pushing my film. I felt like I had just been punched in the gut and was fighting for air. I tried to explain how my efforts had been for the Somaly Mam Foundation and not under the guise of a promotional undertaking, but I was so stunned that I couldn't find very convincing words, I guess. I was filled with emotion because I didn't feel like I had done anything wrong. But I tried to take it all with a grain of salt. I figured that whoever was putting on the event hadn't travelled extensively through parts of the world where sex slavery was common and just didn't understand the cause's importance.

My night turned out great anyway. I had dinner with an amazing woman named Kristina Santa, whom I knew from when I lived in Santa Monica. Kristina is a Southern girl with a tireless work ethic and a smile that never turns upside down. She had just arrived in L.A. a few weeks before me and had been approached by a film crew to host a short documentary called *Spirituality L.A.* We've stayed in touch ever since, and because she's such an open spirit, I can always call her with suggestions for what I could be doing to better my life or make more of a contribution to the world. She's like the sister I never had, and not a day goes by that I don't hold her close to my heart and pray for her success. After dinner that night, we read Napoleon Hill together for hours.

The next day, I visited Agape with Kristina and we saw

the Rev perform live. Wow! Watching him washed away the pain I felt from the night before. Listening to him and his beautiful wife Ricky singing to the piano, listening to the Gospel singers, and feeling the audience's energy was like receiving an electrical charge. The Rev just pours forth from his heart all that he feels inside to inspire the masses. He has a gift! Best of all, after his service, he takes time to share his energy and faith with the people who attended. The Rev and I bumped into each other again and exchanged blessings with each other. This weekend was a manifested dream!

I headed back to Vancouver the next day, grateful to have met some wonderful people whom I was positive I would be connected to for the rest of my life. On the flight home, I thought about how far I'd come since that first day of filming. One day, I had dreamed about making a documentary travel show, and then some powerful force had led me to my true purpose in life.

Coming home, I put out to the universe my need for guidance in what my next step should be. I still felt unsafe in Vancouver. I knew that, for the most part, I was the one creating the story in my mind, but I was hearing an inner voice saying, "Get out now!" My parents understood. I had been on the run for over a year and I needed some stability. I needed a life. I'd heard that sometimes we get introduced to our other self through times of emergencies and distress. I knew it wasn't a coincidence when I felt myself being guided by powers projecting themselves through me. I had worked so intensely on the film that I didn't feel comfortable now having idle time on my hands. I had always believed, "If you want something bad enough, go get it!" I loved to write, but I had been slacking on my daily blogs. I had two voices in my ears. One saying just to pack up the *Return to Happiness* project because the work was done and it was over. The other telling me to get re-focused and use my imagination. That's when my higher self picked up my laptop and started putting my truth into writing this book, and not only did I have a new goal, but it was therapeutic.

Just like any undertaking in life, I knew that promoting *Return to Happiness* wasn't always going to be smooth sailing. I had to understand that the effort I and the people I had allied myself with over the past few years was, in the main, to teach me about the word *happiness*! What happiness is supposed to feel like and how its essence is best learned through adversity. The most important thing I had learned was that acquiring happiness is an inside job. All the people I had met along my path had generally come to the same conclusion. All we have to do is take a look around us, give ourselves the time to breath fresh air, appreciate the good moments, and be grateful for whatever we can learn when bad experiences come in as we let them roll like water over our conscious minds; any emotions that arise from bad experiences we are meant to feel as part of the human experience. If we don't feel bad emotions, how can we appreciate the times of joy and bliss? Since this present moment is really all we have, is there really any sense in worrying? I'm sure many of you have heard the saying, "We are spiritual beings living a human experience." Whatever we are, I believe we are magnificent creatures, all here to create and manifest our dreams. And for the people who need our help in our own and other countries, every little bit we do helps, and it's even better if you can get physically involved. That's where the real fulfillment lies. To see the eyes of people less fortunate look up at you and just to feel their love, their intention…no words have to be said.

I decided now to refocus my energy on writing a book to accompany the *Return to Happiness* film. That way, I could spread the message of happiness in two different mediums and reach even more people. No more idle time for me.

CHAPTER 7
CAR TROUBLES AND DIVINE ORDER

In early September, I went to the Okanagan, in the interior of British Columbia. My parents used to take me to the Okanagan when I was a boy, and clear as day, I can remember building sandcastles on the lake there with my brother. There was no place in the world I loved more. The people there are so down to earth, and since I've always felt connected to nature, the Okanagan's setting in the midst of beautiful mountains and lakes has always made it special for me. I played the best days of my junior hockey experience there, and now my sixth sense guided me there to write a book. Something about being surrounded by the lakes and mountains made it easier for me to channel my creative endeavors.

While in the Okanagan, I met some very special native aboriginal people who had made my stay interesting to say the least. They introduced me to a sacred ceremony centered around a native sweat lodge. I had heard from some good friends in the area that the ceremony was intended to purify the soul and that the sweat lodge was designed to represent the "womb of mother earth." The lodge was large enough for thirty people to fit inside comfortably. The experience takes a lot of courage because intense heat surrounds the "womb" with seven different "grandfather lava rocks" that have been heated in a fire for many hours.

At this particular lodge, there were four rounds of "praying to spirit." The first of the four rounds was a purification round where the pores would open and we would begin to sweat. Any newcomers to the sacred circle would be welcomed with love and prayers offered for their intentions of why they were choosing to take part in the ceremony. Tobacco offerings were given to the elders who led different prayer songs, giving whoever was open to the spirits a direct channel to connect to his higher self. The individual was only allowed to walk around the fire clockwise. The first round of purification could last up to half an hour in intense heat that every individual would try to block out with prayer. The more sincere the desire to connect to spirit, the less the heat would affect the individual. I loved the positive energy in the womb, and I was astonished the first time I was in the lodge because I felt beams of light shooting through my chest. I could see my heart actually beating outside my chest and all I could feel was love. I had a conversation with my late grandfather, who was on my left shoulder, surrounded in white light. I was hot, but so open that at no other time in my life had I experienced such a rush of pure bliss.

I could hear Napoleon Hill's voice in my ears, telling me, "Ryan, you are here in this time to spread the message that we are all unified globally through a oneness of love." When I looked at my left arm, I saw an eagle's wing! I could actually see every feather vein on the wing. "Certainly, this is happening to others," I thought. I was well-hydrated and sober as a bell. But I was seeing visions and insights of past childhood experiences and the Golden Age we have here and now before our eyes.

I knew I was there for training. The mind has to be very strong to last through the ceremony's four rounds. People who weren't fully connected to their spirit would get out in pain. During the second round, we prayed and sang for all the male aspects of our lives. That meant all past relatives and anyone to whom we wanted to reach out. A lot of emotions were shared that first night in the lodge. The third round was prayer to all the female aspects of our lives, and after each individual was done, he would pass off to the next person delegated to pray by saying "to all my relations." The fourth round was GRATITUDE! That was when everyone would pray as one. That round involved the most force and energy. By then, we were all very hot. When it was over, we all would jump into the cool lake, to connect with nature's elements. Then an amazing feast was held for the after ceremony, prepared by wonderful and giving people to celebrate and show respect for what we had just experienced.

I started attending the sweat lodge ceremonies on a weekly basis. Each time when I emerged, the atmosphere would look different; the moon, to which I had always felt very connected, would shine brighter, and overall, I felt safe and protected. I would still be sweating up to two hours later. And the dreams I had were more vivid than ever. I could hear my soft hidden voice that was guiding my every move.

A couple of months after I started visiting the sweat lodge, I was on my way to Kelowna, BC and the countryside sanctuary where I planned to reside in peace and tranquility to write my book. That morning, I was also going to feed the homeless at the local Friendship Center. I always feel a sense of worth when I can give homeless people inspiration. I don't have to throw them money. I can cook them pancakes and connect with them eye-to-eye. I can tell them about my past. And I can hug them and let them know they are loved. Those who feed the homeless often do so because they have been on the other side of the tracks themselves. Plus, it's good old-fashioned fun to make food in the big kitchen as a team, and it's great to see the smiling, happy faces of people after a hot meal.

But this day God had different plans for me! I was driving in the middle of the country with a friend, ready to hop on the grill and get down to business, when my fan belt and water pump broke. I wasn't thrilled because I had just bought the truck a month earlier. Luckily, I was able to glide my vehicle into a nearby gas station's parking lot.

Then something happened. Without feeling any anger or frustration about the situation, I reached back for my new journal, which I had just purchased a few days before. I wrote down on the top of the page "November 25, 2012 (truck breakdown)." Then I started to write about how much I appreciated the experience. In no time, like my truck was a magnet, I had seven different people asking me whether I needed help. I know I must have sent out, through positive thought waves, the desire to have my truck running again. And just like magic, within half an hour, there was a mechanic to analyze the problem. One man was able to get me discounts on a few necessary parts. One gentleman was even kind enough to offer me one of his spare cars. At the end of my journal entry, I expressed gratitude with the word NAMASTE. I don't know why I wrote that word down, but I did. Maybe because subconsciously, I believed in the power of its peaceful meaning.

My truck got fixed after a long day in the cold. Later, I had a few discussions with friends, laughing that this event was for some higher good to lead me more closely down the path upon which I was aligned. After all, I had given a copy of *Return to Happiness* to everyone who came into my experience that day, so who knew what might come from that. Well, one of the people I gave the film to was Emil, a goodhearted man from my first contact with him. He had been willing to help me, and it just so happened that his wife, Marlene, was an enthusiast of New Thought philosophy. In my mind, "new thought" is "old thought"—thought is eternal and always has been. New thought is bringing the old thought, or all that is, into the mainstream of people's focus.

After Emil and Marlene watched the film, she sent me a very heartfelt email saying she "needed" me to meet a friend of hers, Carman; Marlene thought we would have a connection. Of course, I was open to it, so Carman and I spoke the following day after we were introduced on Facebook. When I visited her house, I saw that she had all my favorite books. We spoke the same language I guess you could say. We connected on a soul level, as if she were the sister I'd never had. I felt love radiating from her physical body. Carman and I had a great talk that night, and we both laughed about how my broken down truck engine had synchronized our meeting.

That evening, Carman asked me, "Have you ever heard of Kevin Hall? He wrote an amazing book called *Aspire*." I hadn't heard of Kevin, so Carman placed an autographed copy of his book into my hands. I always hold a book for a minute so I can feel its energy permeate into my hands and determine whether it holds value. Maybe this process doesn't work for everyone, but it works for me. When I read the back of the book, I saw that it had high praise from globally influential people such as Bob Proctor, who stated that Kevin was in the same league as Napoleon Hill and Og Mandino. This book, without a doubt, was in my hands for a reason.

That night, I started reading *Aspire*. In the first chapter, Kevin explains how we are all on a path. He defines Namaste as "Saluting the Divine within. Saluting what you do best. Saluting your natural gifts and uniqueness."

Suddenly, I knew that I wasn't only reading *Aspire* to get a deeper understanding of what the power of words hold. I felt that in the not-so-distant future, I would have the honor of meeting Kevin himself. I asked the universe if it would align me with Kevin. I have a white board in my kitchen with my life goals written on it so I can see them every day. I don't like to waste time, so I read them and affirm them often! I've said before how I operate the equipment of my brain. I see meetings and events like they have already transpired.

I cut Kevin's picture out of the book's back page and stuck it to my vision board on December 10th right beside the word "happiness." So every day when I passed the board, I didn't have much of a choice but to see my goals and say hello to Mr. Hall. Meanwhile, Carman shared my film on Kevin's Facebook wall in hopes he would watch it. She had met Kevin in 2010 and said it was a must that I meet him. Up to this point, Kevin hadn't watched the film yet, but a very nice girl, Julie Herman, who was being mentored by Kevin and was close with his family, watched it. I got a friend request from Julie the day after the film was posted on Mr. Hall's wall. Julie said she was very inspired by the film and she wanted to connect. Julie resided in Utah, worked as a photographer, and owned a documentary film company called Highlife Studios. We had a great conversation. When I sent her a photo of the journal entry I had written on November 25th, the day of my truck breakdown, she was taken back. That's an understatement actually—during our first phone conversation around December 3rd, she said when we talked, she was struck by an intense rush of white light. She then told me that she really wanted me to meet Kevin Hall.

She told me of an event being put on in San Diego on January 4th that Kevin was hosting. She emailed Kevin and gave him my contact information. The more I looked at Kevin's photo on my board and saw his book on my counter, the more I felt my destiny coming into fruition. Then on December 18th, I got a call from Kevin.

"Is this Ryan "*Return to Happiness*" Phillips?" he asked. "Why, yes, it is," I said. We got acquainted and had a good talk, and then Kevin invited me to be a VIP guest at his Genshai Life Mastery Event, which I accepted with gratitude. I thought to myself, "That didn't take long to manifest," and it had come about through a broken engine. It was yet further proof that when you don't have resistant thoughts and just trust that everything is happening in divine order, nature answers your desires, although often in different ways than you may have intended.

CHAPTER 8
GENSHAI LIFE MASTERY RETREAT

"The talent of success is nothing more than doing what you can do well, and doing well whatever you do without thought of fame. If it comes at all it will come because it is deserved, not because it is sought after."
— Henry Wadsworth Longfellow

I spent ten wonderful days at Christmas with Sadie in Vancouver. Then, on January 2nd, I arrived in San Diego to meet Kevin Hall in person. I really didn't know what to expect. I knew from what Kevin had told me over the phone that this retreat would be a life-transforming event that would propel everyone there to invoke a new way of living with purpose! What is purpose? From my personal perspective, it's being fully engaged and on a path to give the world and ourselves the gifts we all possess as unique individuals. All of us here on earth have been given talents, and it's a travesty when people don't recognize their true untapped potential. I know doing what I love doesn't need to pay me anything at all. I would do it for free and have now for many years. It's having fun doing what you love and sincerely giving the greatest gifts you have to give back to humanity.

I don't know how many people attended the event, but the significance of what I was about to learn was enormous. I was so grateful to be there, and the second I walked into the conference room at the Mission Hills Marriot, I felt a burst of beautiful energy fill the room because so many of the people there had come with open hearts to learn about themselves and others, and they all desired a better world built on love and compassion. I made instant friendships with people who will certainly be part of my personal path for the rest of my life.

Over the course of three days, numerous speakers shared their life experiences and adversities, their success principles, and the tools they used to live a life of fulfillment and purpose. In each speaker, we all saw traits of ourselves. When people are so open and loving, they have the ability to connect on a soul level that makes it easy for other people to understand them.

Kevin had promised me that a lot of magic would take place at this event. He had known it, and how could he not? This master of words just has a way of seeing things in all their beauty. Kevin had also promised everyone that he would be personally greeting all the guests half an hour before the event. When I met Kevin, we both felt we had known each other for many years. That night, Kevin, his lovely wife Sherry, and I had dinner at D-Bar Desserts, a local restaurant owned by Keegan Gerhard, one of the top pastry chefs in the United States. We all agreed that we felt like we had known each other for at least fifteen years. I quickly came to realize that Kevin is fun, loving, compassionate, and has a unique sense of humor. When he speaks, his compassion and emotion strike the audience in a way I've never seen. He is a success because his purpose in life shines wholeheartedly through his unwitting desire to see others find their purpose and gifts that they may have lost or buried over the course of their lives. He had set up this event for that sole purpose—to help people discover their own gifts and purpose.

Chef Keegan Gerhard was one of the speakers over the course of the next few days, and let me tell you, he's an amazingly powerful speaker who drives home his message of persistence and self-will to the listener in great ways. He shared his story of personal adversity, loss of a loved one, and how his success resulted from serving others in a respectable way. He wants every one of his customers to leave with an awesome dining experience. I was honored to hear Keegan speak and share his gifts with us.

That first day when I walked alone into the conference room, I saw a woman and her husband carrying a beautiful silver statue of two hands reaching toward each other in an embrace. The lady carrying the statue had an exuberant energy about her. She was filled with love; there was no resistance, and it wouldn't be long before I was introduced to her. Leesa Price and her husband Gary, one of the top sculptors in the United States, had been working on a project that meant the world to them. The small statue I saw was a replica of a larger version that will stand for eternity on the West Coast of the United States called the Statue of Responsibility; it will be three hundred feet tall, the same height as the Statue of Liberty. What a great project for two of the most authentic people I've ever met to be involved in. I was so impressed with the statue that I asked Gary to tell me in his own words, for this book, how it came to be:

> "That which is to give light must endure burning." I love that quote by Viktor Frankl, and I had no idea how much both the author and that quote would play out in my life.

Viktor and I became vicariously acquainted in 1997, the very year of his passing. Kevin Hall had sought me out as a sculptor to realize Viktor's dream of a "Statue of Responsibility." Kevin had had a close working relationship with Stephen R. Covey for many years and had trained Covey's staff for over twenty years. I didn't realize it at the time, but Stephen knew Viktor Frankl, and in fact, Viktor and his famous book *Man's Search For Meaning* were very influential in Stephen writing his famous book *The 7 Habits of Highly Effective People*! And now, sixteen years later, that chain of influence has continued with Kevin Hall writing a bestseller entitled *Aspire*.

So the chronology of the Statue of Responsibility is: Viktor Frankl—Stephen Covey—Kevin Hall—Gary Lee Price.

Kevin recounts the story that he, and his friends Stephen Covey and Dave Newman, realized more than ever at Viktor's passing, that there was a tremendous need in our country for a monument to RESPONSIBILITY. Viktor's idea for a monument to bookend the Statue of Liberty on the East Coast of America with a Statue of Responsibility on the West Coast had yet to be designed, and they were determined to seek out a sculptor of like mentality to bring this noble idea to pass. Kevin said he knew he was on the right track in his search when he first pulled up to my studio and saw that we were loading into the delivery truck a five-foot version of a bronze sculpture I had recently completed and entitled "SYNERGY." Synergy was a key word and concept in the Covey empire. My "SYNERGY" sculpture depicts six interlocking hands forming a circle of unity and working together.

During our visit, Kevin told me of this famous holocaust survivor who had recently passed away without his dream of fully uniting humanity being realized. Kevin proceeded to tell me of this amazing man and his story of not only survival but of victory and massive influence for good. I was astounded by Viktor's trials and challenges at the door of death and despair, and I could not help but think of some of my own experiences. I immediately felt a kinship and brotherhood to this man in our mutual connection to Germany. I had lost my mother and stepfather in a gory scene of murder-suicide at the age of six in Mannheim. More than ever as Kevin recounted Viktor's story, I realized that not only do we all have trials and challenges, but it's what we *do* with those challenges that defines who we really are as humans.

I told Kevin in front of my studio that beautiful fall day in 1997 that I was up to the challenge and felt like I had had enough of life's challenges and experiences that I could come up with a design that would have significant impact and meaning.

As I set about the task of creating a clay study for a future 300-foot monument, I did a lot of reflection on my body of work as a sculptor and what it was that I really wanted to say. What would I visually want to leave the planet if I could use *my* voice to say that which I truly felt represented RESPONSIBILITY? My mantra as a sculptor had been "Lifting the Human Spirit through Sculpture." I wanted the piece to be able to make an instant statement of my core values as a human, my deepest beliefs. In my research, I also came up with the idea that visually and architecturally, the shape and message must be simple and very recognizable. I did not want any room for abstract theory or interpretation—I wanted my statement bold and powerful. As I sifted through these thoughts and ideas, and reflected upon my past work, I saw some patterns emerge. Many of my pieces depicted figures in tandem, whether they were birds, animals, or humans. And the human figures depicted interaction, connection, flight, and upward mobility. It was a great exercise in self-discovery to realize what my core values really were. Above all, my message to humanity would have to do with relationships! How and if that related to "responsibility" I knew not—but I did know in order to be true and give integrity to my voice—it had to depict relationships. My fundamental belief is that all things in life boil down to them. I did not realize until later that my simple, vertical, rectangular shape of two clasped hands was somehow divinely connected to Viktor Frankl and what his VISUAL core values were!

In 2004, I was part of a small entourage of Americans who ended up in Vienna, Austria, ringing the door buzzer of the very apartment from where Viktor and his family, some sixty years earlier, had been snatched. Viktor's first wife, Tilly, and inborn child, had died in the Nazi concentration camp along with his parents. Elly, Viktor's second wife and lifelong assistant, answered the door and let her prearranged visitors enter what we all felt was sacred space. We immediately sensed not only the warmth of the flat but also the shrine that this home was to learning and knowledge. Elly was a spry seventy-seven-year-old, delightful little lady who spoke fluent English with a beautiful German accent. Little did I realize just how spry Elly was until we went walking around Vienna on that very cold but significant November day. We visited a park after her husband's namesake and the Jewish cemetery where Viktor lies.

After very warm and gracious introductions, we were invited into even more sacred space—Viktor's library and study—or I should say, one of Viktor's libraries, as there were books everywhere!

We unveiled the seventeen-inch stainless steel Statue of Responsibility study that I had cast from my clay studio creation. Mrs. Frankl took the piece in her hands, and after thoughtful consideration, she said to me, "May I show you Viktor's favorite piece of sculpture?" He had two pieces of art that he treasured—a sculpture and a drawing. Elly pointed toward one of her husband's bookshelves. She said that Viktor had come across this sculpture shortly after he had gotten out of the prison camps; it had meant so much to him that he put it on "layaway" since he could not completely pay for it at the time. She said it was one of his only treasures, and that he'd had a "niche" created in the middle of this particular bookshelf for its display. She said Viktor entitled this antique wood carving "The Suffering Man" and used it as a metaphor for our relationships to our fellow man and would ask the question, "Where is the hand reaching down?" Being a tactile, touchy guy, I asked Elly if I could hold the sculpture, fully realizing its intrinsic value.

She gave me the nod of approval with a distinct "Ja, naturlich" as I reached into the leather-padded niche and plucked it from its nesting quarters. Who knows how long it had rested there, undisturbed? She said that sculpture was Viktor's visual for the concept of RESPONSIBILITY and that our obligation toward each other was "humanistic" rather than purely theoretical.

That was cause not only for me in my heart of hearts to celebrate—but for all of us as we shortly celebrated Viktor and my like-mindedness at a quaint but popular little restaurant where Beethoven had completed his ninth symphony and other musical masterpieces during his trials of old age and deafness. It was very apropos as Kevin had us all go around, from person to person, and recount the chain of events that led us to that epic moment! I will never forget that confirmation that somehow, someway, all the elements of space and time had come together to create a monument so much needed for our times. And since that inspired rendezvous on a cold and chilly November Viennese evening, times have even made it more clear that, as another heralded and celebrated victor, Victor Hugo, pointed out "NOTHING IS MORE POWERFUL THAN AN IDEA WHOSE TIME HAS COME!"

Indeed the time is now, and marvelous things have aligned themselves and come together for this historical event to happen. Its roots are deep—it's not just one man's idea or just an artist's concept—it is about ALL of us and our obligation and responsibility to each other as a united and cohesive, loving human family. I love my wife

> Leesa's visionary statement: It's not just about creating a MONUMENT; it's about creating a MOVEMENT!
> — Gary Lee Price, sculptor

As people told their stories, Kevin sat in the back like a Zen master. He watched and listened, just as much in awe as everyone else while we became educated in how to live a life built on purpose. Kevin smiled wisely many times over the course of the three days because he could see people becoming awakened and inspired to an unlimited stream of untapped potential. One thing Kevin said that really stood out in my mind was "You are never better than you think you are, and you can do more than you think you can!" God, do I believe that. It's the action we perform from our hearts and the scope we create in our loving imagination that allows us to succeed and make a difference in life!

A few other things Kevin drove into our minds and that really resonated with me were:

- I commit. I will not quit!
- Work is a form of worship when performed with passion and purpose.
- The best way to heal a broken heart is to put it back to work with passionate meaningful labor that serves others.
- Act as if it were impossible to fail.

I could write a full book about the rest of this event, but I'll just mention a few of the people who really inspired me and I believe will be part of my life-creating dreams for ever.

Gary, the master sculptor, guided us through forming our vision for the next year. With all his earnestness and his eyes closed, he allowed us to tap into the creative faculties of our imagination. I saw colors, I saw travel and giving, but most of all, I saw giving back to the world through the inner child in my heart. So I tried my best to form out of clay my small childlike hand with a heart in the middle. That's what came to mind, and that's the gift that Gary made me see, feel, and mold, all through energy. Everyone had a masterpiece in his or her own right. What didn't surprise me in the least was that everyone wanted to contribute more to this world. Thank you, Gary, for letting me see it. And thank you all for making me believe it. We all create. Creation is what got us here, and it's what we consciously or unconsciously continue to do.

When I met Sean Stephenson in the lobby with his dad, I had no idea he was there to speak. I just saw this happy-go-lucky dude roll into the lobby in his wheelchair with self-confidence and dignity. I was obviously drawn to him and we had a little conversation, the first of what would be many in the next few days. Sean has a rare bone disease called osteogenesis imperfecta, commonly known as "brittle bone disease." Most of his bones were broken during his birth. Doctors warned that he might not survive. But he did! And he's here for a mighty big reason. His growth was stunted and he stands just over three feet tall. But in the eyes of millions, he stands before the world as a giant!

Sean has been a public motivational speaker since the age of seventeen with the assistance of the Make-A-Wish Foundation. In 1998, he met his idol, Tony Robbins, who would become his mentor and encourage him to work on his health to reduce his constant breaking of bones. Sean explained to me that he had broken over two hundred bones. He would be planning to do something like go on a trip when he would break a collarbone. That would be some adversity to overcome for anyone. But Sean's light shines as bright as the largest star. Later when I heard Sean speak from his heart, I had tears in my eyes. Despite his adversities, he told us how he had worked as an intern for

President Bill Clinton and for Illinois Congressman Bill Lipinski. He received a bachelor's degree in political science in 2001 and has published two books: *How You(th) Can Succeed!: Transforming Dreams into Reality for Young Adults*, and most recently, *Get Off Your 'But': How to End Self-Sabotage and Stand Up for Yourself.* I won't disclose what Sean charges for his energetic speaking talent that moves mountains, but it's worth every penny. Sean has been on Oprah and many other shows, sharing his message of inspiration. He is a YouTube sensation, and I highly recommend watching some of his real life lessons delivered with passion. During his talk that day, Sean emphasized how *action* is the solution—to listen to more than what you need to hear, meditate twenty minutes each day, get eight hours of sleep, and my favorite, "Don't wait because you just don't know!"

Sean is a happy man; he doesn't want anyone to feel sorry for him! His greatest gift is to make people realize that it's the human spirit that truly matters. He tells people to let go of snap judgments—if they see a flaw in him, it's only a mirror reflection of something they see in themselves.

Later, Sean and I talked about life, and we danced as a group, Sean with his Boombox under his wheelchair. And believe me, he was the one most dancing up a storm. Sean has taken everything he was born with and turned his life into one of inspiration and purpose. Thank you for being you, Sean Stephenson.

Another couple I met who exemplified courage, comeback, and the willingness to share their tragedy with their hearts wide open were Sean Fleming and his lovely wife, Cologne. When they had met in 1991, they had become instant sweethearts and soon were married. Cologne had a two-year-old son named Canyon, whom Sean adopted as his own, and Sean and Cologne went on to have more children. Then an event happened that would change their lives forever. When Canyon was sixteen, he found a gun in Sean's closet. Canyon died of a gunshot wound. Sean and Cologne would never know if it were an accident or Canyon had intended to commit suicide. No one who has not personally undergone such a tragedy can have any idea of the pain and suffering that parents put on themselves in these cases.

Sean had recently published a book called *Lost Canyon*, a riveting and healing book about grief and recovery. I was honored to meet Sean and his wife, and I know our paths crossed for a very important reason. When Gary Price gave us the task of molding our clay, Sean and I created the same miniature sculpture. Many reasons flashed into my mind for why we both created it. My miniature art piece was a replica of my hand with a heart in the middle, signifying that I intended to give to the world the heart of my inner child over the course of the next year. While I don't victimize myself anymore, at times, I still feel like I was robbed of my inner child, but I realize it was all for the greater good—so I would now stand for helping kids, letting people reach out for help, and being a voice for others. And that's what Sean and Cologne Fleming are—they are now there to help anyone contemplating suicide.

Sean and Cologne are humble; they have shown that a family can rebuild, and they are a huge example of how it's done—through acceptance and their full faith that their son Canyon's energy is in a good place. Energy never dies. So it's the precious moments that they remember. Sean has taught me more than he realizes—that no matter how bad the going gets, we are here to live in the present.

Harvey Mackay, author of the *New York Times* bestseller *Swim with the Sharks Without Being Eaten Alive*, was another phenomenal speaker. At age eighty, he has the energy of a twenty-year-old, and his magnetic personality is amazing to watch. His sustainability is due to staying healthy and constantly active. He is a great thinker and a true pro on the business of people. Among his words of wisdom was always to keep a rolodex for your connections. Contacts are what it's all about when you need specialized knowledge in any business. He made it crystal clear the importance of a mastermind alliance, something I was already familiar with from reading Napoleon Hill. He has shared his life experience with millions through his books and business alliances and has attracted the friendship of such great people as Mohammed Ali and TV host Larry King.

I'm citing these people because they are such inspiring examples of how temporary setbacks and obstacles are simply tests. They are all testaments to how faith and self-discipline will allow you to gain purpose in your life.

The last day of the retreat, I told Kevin how I had manifested my desire to meet him through writing about it and using his photo. Kevin loved what I had to say and asked me to share it with the group. The audience was receptive to me. When I explained how an intangible thought can truly reproduce itself into its physical counterpart and I used my desire to meet Kevin as an example, everyone was a bit taken aback by how successfully my plan had worked, but they knew from having met me that I was speaking the truth. I also shared that portion of the rough draft of this book with Kevin and autographed it for him. When he read it, he told me I could write—imagine that—a kid who didn't apply himself all through high school, didn't even read a book, a drop-out. Now my life was one of specialized knowledge that I was privileged to share with others. Education is an amazing thing when it's taught with passion and purpose. Once I found what interested me, I had proven there was no end to the learning I could acquire and the action I could take. So I urge everyone to take his or her own unique path. Just follow your bliss! Smile in the mirror and feel the life force coming out of you in each sacred heartbeat.

After the retreat was over, I rented a car in San Diego to go and see my friend at Joshua Tree National Park. The day after, I made a quick stop at Agape to give the Rev a big hug and talk to the staff about the book I was finishing. Then that afternoon, I met with a video distribution company in Beverly Hills to have an in-depth conversation about *Return to Happiness.*

I almost didn't get to the airport in time for my 7:30 p.m. flight back to Vancouver because the traffic was so bad, but in the end, I made it. As I settled into my seat on the plane, I was anxious to get back into nature, where I felt I could best put the finishing touches on my book. I had my goals set from the Kevin Hall retreat, and I had another bike ride in February for the Somaly Mam Foundation that I had to get into shape for—mentally, spiritually, and physically. I thought about the dividends my dad had said I would receive the day he told me I was free to enter the U.S. again. I knew now what those dividends were. I knew what he had meant and what I desired. I desired to meet amazing people who were making huge contributions to the world by sharing their unique gifts and giving back. Really, it's a gift just to be able to give back!

I knew I would be in L.A. again in April—that was the goal. This was the end to new beginnings in my life. The next time I would see the United States would be after another wild bike ride in Southeast Asia. Time, space, and the reality that we all have here makes me want to answer the never-ending question of how limited are we? Unlimited, infinite…able just to keep creating. For me, I would create more Happiness, and I had been blessed to receive a lot of it.

CONCLUSION
NEW BEGINNINGS WITHOUT END

Happiness is something most people desire. Each individual, however, can measure it very differently. Growing up in the West, I know how much emphasis is put on career status and materialism. Men are measured by so many cheap opinions about how much money they have, how nice of a car, or how big of a house they own. Having the nice luxuries of life isn't a bad thing at all, but when we can connect from an inner perspective with more people as brothers and sisters of the human race, that's where happiness can be waiting for all of us.

The thing most people fail to realize is that everything is temporary. There are only three things in life we can't change: other people's opinions, the weather, and change itself. It's a travesty to watch people overeat, over-sex, and tread the mill of life with no purpose. People who have a purpose find that their happiness comes easily because they are always engaged in doing what they love. I know that doing what I love doesn't need to pay me much. As long as

I can have friends who are like family, my world is always filled with peace of mind and contentment. Wouldn't this world be a better place if people were all treated as equals? I urge everyone who reads this book to have a passion for practicing compassion. Gandhi said, "Be the change you want to see in the world." Wars generate money and deaths. The majority of people are always looking for the easy way out. If they are feeling bad, they believe there's always a fix in the form of a pill or drink.

If you're a person who finds it hard to love others, try loving yourself first. This universe is nothing short of perfection—just like you. The laws of the universe are so precise that if we just align ourselves with them, our true nature will be so natural and free because that's where we came from in the first place. Television, films, and magazines are right in our faces about how we should act and look. It's important to keep our own individuality and stay true to ourselves. The true leaders of today are the ones who separate themselves from the crowds and aren't afraid to be themselves. True leadership comes through thinking for oneself; being fearless and relentless in the pursuit of goals keeps the mind always at work with an intention. If you don't have a goal, I'm sure there's something you want badly enough that you can write it down on paper and make it your dominating dream. Just remember that we are the ones in control of our destinies. And if you're going to emulate someone, emulate the great!

As the days go by and I really look inside my soul, I see why I went on this journey. I see that every person came into my experience because I was aware of the full intention of the *Return to Happiness* project. I kept it fun and happy. Although I had to surmount many obstacles through the waves of life, it was all for the greater good. I know now that because there is no end to the expanding universe, it's so important to be healthy, love lots, decide what you want to do, and make the conscious decision to be as happy as you can be. The experience of creating the film and writing the book for *Return to Happiness* has attracted amazing like-minded people into my life. Sometimes, life can be strange, but I know more than ever that the power within our hearts and imagination is capable of creating anything.

I'm positive of another thing as well—that in order to receive fully all the blessings in life, we need to give as well. Today, more than at any other time in history, people are realizing this universal truth—that you get what you give! I know that every day I want to return to happiness and take as many people with me on the journey as possible. As I write these words, it's just a few days before I fly to Hong Kong on February 4th, and three days later, I will take off with thirteen other riders for the BIG RIDE of 2013. This time, the ride starts in Siegon, Vietnam. We will pedal 545 kilometers to Angkor Wat. This year there will be fewer riders, but I'll ride with more purpose. I know this group can raise some money and contribute. I can feel it in my bones. I'm committed.

I will be riding on behalf of all the riders from last year and this year, and for Somaly Mam, the girls, the entire foundation, and, of course, so we all may find more inner happiness in our lives. What a ride, what an adventure, and what a kick it will be to raise some money for the cause before we jump on our bikes and wind through Vietnam and Cambodia. I'm so looking forward to seeing all the wonderful people I met last year, and all the new people who have love in their hearts.

I will also be riding this year for my friend, Terry Enright. While I was in L.A. editing the film, I had talked to Terry. He told me he wouldn't be there for the 2013 bike ride because he'd had two heart attacks, but he was positive and said, "I believe in you, Ryan. Keep going on with what you're doing." Two weeks later, I found out he had made his transition into the non-physical. But his light and spirit will shine down on the riders and the world as inspiration and love for eternity.

More than ever now, I've finally been able to accept that my hockey career wasn't supposed to happen for a reason. My intuition guided me out of the darkness. I have seen the light about the drug business that can have serious consequences. I'm alive today; I made it to where I am now so I could create the person I intend to be. To be someone who can just accept the feelings coming into his body and mind. To know that I can just be real and so can everyone else if he or she chooses. Today, I choose to be happy; it's a really simple choice. I could feel sorry for myself and others, but what good is that going to do for anyone? Now I stand for something—I stand for giving my love and humble advice to whoever wants to hear it. I didn't know until writing this book that I had packed so much life experience into forty years. Now I get the gift of still being a kid—of playing in the world. No wonder I feel so free on a bike. It always takes me back to when I was that little boy with his whole life ahead of him. The same little guy who has the same spirit now, just in a bigger body with a bit more hard-earned wisdom.

In closing, my journey of life wouldn't have been possible if it weren't for all the ups and downs, turns and twists, curveballs and close calls I've encountered. I hope, like me, you can make today and every day one that counts for something. If you follow some of the suggestions presented in this book, I promise a great shift for you. It takes sacrifice, but it is so well worth it. I challenge each and every one of you to stand for good. To leave better off not only every person and group you come into contact with, but to leave this world a better place for generations to come. We all have the choice when we awaken each day to give all we can, to leave no rocks unturned, and to know that nothing ever happens without intention and action! Remember, happiness is a state of mind that we all possess, and in every heart, we have the power to make a positive change in the world. And just know that no matter where you are in the world, I'm sending my happiness, love, and compassion every step of the way.

Returning other people's lives to happiness is something we can all do on a daily basis! Sometimes in life, it's the people we think don't need a boost of good energy, who need it the most. But most important is never to stop trying. Our authentic selves always know exactly what we need to keep going. Through any kind of healing, there is sure to be pain. I don't think growing pains ever really end; that's all part of evolutionary growth. The past few years have been an interesting adventure, continuing to meet new people and expand my awareness. In 2015, I was diagnosed with being bi-polar, a mental condition that millions of people in the world suffer from. I choose to fight back naturally, but I realize that some people's mental illnesses are so severe that medication is a necessity. I don't mean to minimize the importance of certain kinds of medicine, and I wish to see the day mental illness can be cured naturally. My medication comes in the form of exercise and keeping busy with projects that stimulate my mind. Associating with compassionate beings who accept me for who I am keeps the motor running smoothly in the majority of cases. But don't we all choose either to embrace the days of suffering or turn them into building blocks of joy?

I'm eternally grateful to the people who supported me during my time in prison. I had so many good coaches along the way as well, who instilled timeless knowledge. The now is what matters always, and today, I'm so enthused to be participating in a rapidly growing generation of higher consciousness. Acceptance of my own inner being has led me into the inner spheres of the universal domain. The manifestations that blossom are always a mirror reflection of our thoughts from the heart. Ethical business, if we want it, is soaring its way onto the leading edge of thought, and success will follow with loving intention. It's all about bringing people together who desire abundance that is created on the higher planes of evolution. A new brand of leadership is at the forefront for people who want not only a better world, but better results.

This past year, after hearing about so many unnecessary deaths due to mental illness, I decided to embark on another journey. This journey, because of my diagnoses that I may be bi-polar or suffering from post-trauma from my younger days, is a sensitive one in my heart. I have decided to ride my bike across Canada with my great friend and brother Jay for the sole purpose of raising funds and awareness for mental health. Jay's story is a miracle, just like all of our stories; he was run over by thirteen train cars in 2008. Jay was left for dead on the tracks and lost a leg and foot in the tragedy. Induced into a coma for five weeks while fighting for his life, he now lives to give back hope through positive action. He too has converted suffering into motivation, and I'm proud to have such an inspiration ride alongside me. Mental illness is a debilitating disease that affects too many people, many of them close to me. I will be leaving on July 1st 2016 with love in my heart for the people in the world who suffer from all forms of mental illness. I believe the stigma needs to come to an end, and it's okay to reach out. I feel it's my duty to continue my humanitarian work, only this time, North America's roads will be the ones I travel. ONEMIND CYLCE is intended to help those in need and once again prove that with the power of belief…anything is possible.

ABOUT THE AUTHOR

Ryan John Phillips is actively involved in his community of Vancouver, British Columbia, Canada, and in the world with public speaking engagements that uplift the human spirit. Ryan prides himself on delivering compelling real life stories to show that we can all be vulnerable and our true selves. His zest for life and helping to motivate others achieve their dreams always comes across through his enthusiastic approach to give all he's got to a large audience or individual. When Ryan has spare time, he loves to play hockey, golf, hike, and give all he's got to being of service to others. For more info on Ryan, feel free to check out his websites and social media outlets and perhaps he can help you. *Return To Happiness*, the documentary, can be watched for free on YouTube. Ryan is a featured TEDx StanleyPark speaker in May of 2016 as well, where he addresses the issue of Children for Sale.

www.returntohappiness.com
www.ryanjohnphillips.com
www.onemindcycle.com

Twitter @RyanJohn88
Instagram RYANPHILLIPS888

Facebook
Return To Happiness
Ryan John Phillips
OneMind Cycle